WELCOME TO LEARN GERMAN
WITH WORD

Learning a new language ca
book provides puzzle based ... exercises and is intended to
supplement traditional methods of language study. We believe that
learning should be fun. If you are doing something that you enjoy,
then it will be easy to stick with.

In Learn GERMAN with Word Search Puzzles you will find a collection
of 130 bilingual word search puzzles that will challenge you with
dozens of interesting categories.

This book includes:
• Diverse categories including: Numbers, Colors, The Body, Weather,
Professions, Fruits, Vegetables, Verbs, Opposites, and many more!
• Words hidden horizontally, vertically or diagonally in each puzzle
• Easy to read puzzles
• Challenging and fun!
• Puzzle based learning provides unique learning perspective
• 65 jumbled review puzzles to challenge your memory and lock in
those translations with reinforcement learning
• Complete solutions provided.

Keep your Mind Active and Engaged
Studies have shown that continuously challenging your brain with
puzzles and games or acquiring new skills such as a new language can
help to delay symptoms of dementia and Alzheimer's. Keeping a
sharp mind is great idea for people of any age.

Learn with Word Search Series
Revised and updated for 2018.
Now include 10 challenging languages. Check out our other titles!

Happy searching!

To those who occasionally struggle to find the correct words.

Welcome to Learn with Word Search. It's time to count down to your new vocabulary. Here we go. Three. Two. One Find these number translations in the grid below.

```
T H I R T E E N E F E S A E N I
T T R O O L Ö N E E C X N N E L
T H R E E N I N I Y A V Ü E E E
Ö C G V N E E F V Y Z O E I T W
R A E I U H W M R O A W N T R O
N N T F E G Z V Q I H R Ö N U A
W S F Ü N F Z S D O T Z O L O Y
O L T E N A H S B R H L H Ö F L
A N V B A C V V W X P G S O C A
M E V L E W T I J B Ü P U D E C
S E S S N D E E N R R A J I Ü
T T A I Ü F O R M R N G A G A W
S F X E E I H Z L K D P Ö O S O
O I T D L B S E N P E O B A R A
A F Ü N F Z E H N O N W H A E H
D R E I Z E H N H E Z T N H A L
```

ONE	EIN
TWO	ZWEI
THREE	DREI
FOUR	VIER
FIVE	FÜNF
SIX	SECHS
SEVEN	SIEBEN
EIGHT	ACHT
NINE	NEUN
TEN	ZEHN
ELEVEN	ELF
TWELVE	ZWÖLF
THIRTEEN	DREIZEHN
FOURTEEN	VIERZEHN
FIFTEEN	FÜNFZEHN

A zillion is often used to describe a huge number, but it doesn't actually have a defined value. We won't make you count to a zillion, but below you will find some more numbers to add to your vocabulary.

```
T A U S E N D H Y T X I S T T S
A S N C O H W G I ß I E R D A E
E G Y T T E D N E B V X A L T C
R C I T T Z T E L E Ü S E I I H
G F B Z Y N A E N E U N Z I G Z
I I E F B U D T R E D N U H N I
Z F Z O W E Y X F F Ü N F Z I G
N T T R R N I I T H O U S A N D
A Y Y D E ß H S A T E L M O E N
W C N T T I M E A Y T R I H T E
Z U H Ü H I V C Z T Y L Y W E E
H E Q T L G H H U B L T E O E T
R N D L Z T I Z X I E N R O N H
N P I H Z E A E M N T I A O J G
A O P I ß G H H I Y Y A S D F I
N L G S E V E N T E E N S T I E
```

SIXTEEN	SECHZEHN
SEVENTEEN	SIEBZEHN
EIGHTEEN	ACHTZEHN
NINETEEN	NEUNZEHN
TWENTY	ZWANZIG
THIRTY	DREIßIG
FORTY	VIERZIG
FIFTY	FÜNFZIG
SIXTY	SECHZIG
SEVENTY	SIEBZIG
EIGHTY	ACHTZIG
NINETY	NEUNZIG
HUNDRED	HUNDERT
THOUSAND	TAUSEND
MILLION	MILLION

The seven days of the week were named after the seven celestial bodies that were visible to the naked eye thousands of years ago. These are the Sun, Moon, Mercury, Venus, Mars, Jupiter, and Saturn. See if you can spot their translations with your naked eye below.

```
N A T I O N A L H O L I D A Y N
R A O Q S S A E M W I S O R E A
G D R E A P H W E E K E N D T T
S U N D A Y S A Q E D W N A U I
G K N S G H E F R A L E E E E O
U A I O L A R S Y P N D R E H N
X M T N T E T A T E T N S D Q A
K M I N I O D S H E E E T Y E L
F O M T O O M C M Y R S A R R F
E R A A T M O O O A A D G M M E
A G I G Y W N I R D S A A V R I
N E W D I D O M N R A Y E Y E E
N N O E A N E C U U O Y T L N R
L T C Y E Y T H H T F W E T L T
G P H P O K T E Y A D S E U T A
N R E T S E G A T S N E I D T G
```

MONDAY	MONTAG
TUESDAY	DIENSTAG
WEDNESDAY	MITTWOCH
THURSDAY	DONNERSTAG
FRIDAY	FREITAG
SATURDAY	SAMSTAG
SUNDAY	SONNTAG
WEEKEND	WOCHENENDE
NATIONAL HOLIDAY	NATIONALFEIERTAG
TODAY	HEUTE
TOMORROW	MORGEN
YESTERDAY	GESTERN
WEEK	WOCHE
DAY	TAG

The Roman calendar originally had ten months, which explains why September, October, November and December are based on the latin words for seven, eight, nine and ten. Search for the months and their translations below.

```
O S O M Ä R Z F E B R U A R Y Ä
D E C E M B E R W E N P E A J J
P P C W J M K B S W R B C D A I
R T L G T U A I M I M R P N H N
E E Y R Q T L A L E A H U E R O
B M A R C H E Y Z U V A M L T V
M B M D L A N E R Ä R O M A I E
E E E B O T D B P Y N I N C N M
T R D P S Y E A R T I O O U G B
P N E U O F R U H S M N J E T E
E R G B P Ä H E S X E H O U E R
S U A S O M S J B F D D U L N T
A U G U S T T B W O E Ä D I A I
H O G G N B K Ä M L T N S W E P
R L I R P A R O Ä Z R C Ä A A S
I L G I L U J E O N N S O E S I
```

JANUARY	JANUAR
FEBRUARY	FEBRUAR
MARCH	MÄRZ
APRIL	APRIL
MAY	MAI
JUNE	JUNI
JULY	JULI
AUGUST	AUGUST
SEPTEMBER	SEPTEMBER
OCTOBER	OKTOBER
NOVEMBER	NOVEMBER
DECEMBER	DEZEMBER
CALENDAR	KALENDER
MONTH	MONAT
YEAR	JAHR

The seasons are caused by the tilt of the Earth as it orbits the sun. For part of the year the sun shines longer on one hemisphere resulting in summer. Tilt your head and search for these words related to time and the seasons below.

```
T L F V L Y R H Ü T M Y I V J S
S A N I G H T A N E O I E D Y T
S N N T J N S E C O N D N A C U
T Y Ü O O Y P M H E A W D U R N
D S O M M E R N M C O I C G T D
A W B J O G I I E E A N R N R E
I S H R B R N D N N S T H I E Z
A R U R E U G I A T P E O L D N
F A I M T H H E N U Z R U H N E
T I Z E M H E D N R N Ü R Ü U F
E D N U K E S E H Y O O B R H N
R E T N I W R A U T U M N F R N
N T Q A R S J D E H N R S O H Z
O I H M G I O Ü F C H I H H A G
O N A C H M I T T A G N L V J M
N T E O F E W O J N E M S X U A
```

WINTER	WINTER
SPRING	FRÜHLING
SUMMER	SOMMER
AUTUMN	HERBST
SECOND	SEKUNDE
MINUTE	MINUTE
HOUR	STUNDE
DAY	TAG
MONTH	MONAT
YEAR	JAHR
MORNING	MORGEN
AFTERNOON	NACHMITTAG
NIGHT	NACHT
DECADE	JAHRZEHNT
CENTURY	JAHRHUNDERT

COLORS

The three primary colors are red, green and blue. These three colors can be combined to create an astonishing variety of color. Astonish yourself by finding these translations in the grid below.

```
A S S S D Ü S V C ß V S ß E I C
E C I N Y I S M U W R E R O H T
Ü H L B L A C K N Y N N G O O H
H W B V U H W S T E N T N S Y S
T A E O H D G L A F P G I H F O
N R R I E O E E R W E L H U ß T
ß Z O O ß E E P H M U C A N A G
V D S ß T E S I B G L L O E R R
E B A N N D T N R ß B N S W O A
T Y L T Ü E A K O N D R O Ü T H
E O I T O R E T W B E L A E P T
S A U U A R G R N T L D O U N X
K E O O O R A N G E L E R G N L
Ü Y M Y C Y A N Y O G P G R N H
S R N H T Y H T G E L A I E P R
T ß D S Z E A T N E G A M Y N A
```

BLACK	SCHWARZ
BLUE	BLAU
BROWN	BRAUN
CYAN	ZYAN
GOLD	GOLD
GREY	GRAU
GREEN	GRÜN
MAGENTA	MAGENTA
ORANGE	ORANGE
PINK	ROSA
PURPLE	LILA
RED	ROT
SILVER	SILBER
WHITE	WEIß
YELLOW	GELB

SHAPES

A dodecagon has 12 sides, while a megagon has a million sides, at which point it is essentially a circle. Time to think outside the box and find these 2D and 3D shapes in the puzzle below.

```
R E D N I L Y Z R T L A V O L H
E R I X E T I C U B E R E H P S
C E L G N A I R T Y G U R K E S
T D I A M O N D T I U A T C N L
A N R E T S G A F U K A H E T C
N I A L F L R A A N O S J T A E
G L D M Ü D C U T K E K E H G A
L Y E Ü A H O G W C C R M C O L
E C H U T I H C K E O O I E N A
D T Q E C W D O I F E B N R O T
I G C N R I V E M N R X H E G U
M K T R M A R S A Ü F N H H A E
A T T A L D U C I F T U I A X L
R Ü R T L T G Q L E F R Ü W E P
Y Y X S L R E I S E R C E I H E
P O B T E N N L E G E K C O S P
```

CIRCLE	KREIS
CONE	KEGEL
CUBE	WÜRFEL
CYLINDER	ZYLINDER
DIAMOND	DIAMANT
HEXAGON	SECHSECK
OCTAGON	ACHTECK
OVAL	OVAL
PENTAGON	FÜNFECK
PYRAMID	PYRAMIDE
RECTANGLE	RECHTECK
SPHERE	KUGEL
SQUARE	QUADRAT
STAR	STERN
TRIANGLE	DREIECK

Our face is the most expressive part of our body. We can convey a variety of emotions with the 43 muscles we have in our face. Below are some words related to your face and head.

```
N D H E S T F C T O N G U E Ä R
O R O O S W O R B E Y E S O N H
X I T L X I R E C V Q S C H A O
S S T H R M E C A F Ä I L I U D
H W H H E P H A A R L C R D G E
A J Y H D E E N T A E H A I E H
E T S S T R A V L A O T A F N T
E G D R T N D A O H L E H M B E
M S N S E I O E Q W D H M Z R O
T O T I O D J S S N A U H U A W
T W U Ä E N H Ä Z A N N N U S
R H S T C E R Ä S D N P G G E I
I H T H H L G I N L I P P E N K
S Q D E E O I U T I K I N O O N
N O O A E Y E L A S H E S P I L
X E Ä D K T E I O R D C F T H P
```

CHEEK	WANGE
CHIN	KINN
EAR	OHR
EYE	AUGE
EYEBROWS	AUGENBRAUEN
EYELASHES	WIMPERN
FACE	GESICHT
FOREHEAD	STIRN
HAIR	HAAR
HEAD	KOPF
LIPS	LIPPEN
MOUTH	MUND
NOSE	NASE
TEETH	ZÄHNE
TONGUE	ZUNGE

The human body is a remarkable thing, with hundreds of specialized parts that we take for granted every day. Here is a list of some important parts of the body to remember.

```
R E G N I F U ß S E E H R W O S
T D A U M E N T H L B D A Ü F C
S A R S D E ß E B S K T Z O E H
C L E E L L B O G E N ß I S R U
E B R U S T W A R Z E O A M L L
W R E H H T Z H N N L B O R ß T
I E E F O N M L H L E T Y Y Ü E
F D L T U N O N A I G E L O I R
I L L E L P P I N I D O X Ü L B
E U I R D U I P D W N O ß F Ü L
E O A K E N H H S E A T ß W E A
F H T T R G A C T T H I I I R T
F S F O T R N H S U T S S M T T
A Ü W O M L L I M G A K S T S C
H E Z F L Ü R B F N H S E Y U T
F A E O F W ß Y W U G V O N H E
```

ARM	ARM
ELBOW	ELLBOGEN
FINGER	FINGER
FOOT	FUß
HAND	HAND
HIP	HÜFTE
LEG	BEIN
NIPPLE	BRUSTWARZE
SHOULDER	SCHULTER
SHOULDER BLADE	SCHULTERBLATT
THUMB	DAUMEN
TOE	ZEH
WAIST	TAILLE
WRIST	HANDGELENK

Skin is the largest human organ and is approximately 15% of your body weight. Search for these other parts of the body and their translations in the puzzle grid below.

```
Ä T M Ü H Ä Ü T C O E É U Ü E T
Ä W A O G A H K E L D I Ä Ä T O
L X Ä H I I T L E B A N L R I E
E L K N A S Ä V M H W K B R V Ü
K C A B K U A Ü H C L I H Z E F
N Ö N I T N T S S O S E C N F U
E K N E E K K I Y S E F F O I U
H D R K É C T V F R Ä I C S N M
C T C E Q E M H O F N S T T G Ü
S Ü O T P N H Ö R G Ø S E P E Y
R L T S U R B I E Ø A R G R T
É U A E J L Ö R A E A H I Ü N Y
B L E H C Ö N R R I T P T A A
O T S F L A C B M G Ü I M O G O
D A O N I F K I H Y E T R R E Z
Y L E L H Ö H L E S H C A Ä L T
```

ANKLE	KNÖCHEL
ARMPIT	ACHSELHÖHLE
BACK	RÜCKEN
BODY	KÖRPER
BREAST	BRUST
BUTTOCKS	GESÄSS
CALF	WADE
FINGERNAIL	FINGERNAGEL
FOREARM	UNTERARM
KNEE	KNIE
NAVEL	NABEL
NECK	HALS
SKIN	HAUT
THIGH	OBERSCHENKEL
THROAT	KEHLE

Our internal organs regulate the body's critical systems, providing us with oxygen and energy, and filtering out toxins. Check out this list of squishy but important body parts.

```
E  Ü  E  E  B  L  I  N  J  P  S  T  N  G  C  S
S  M  A  L  L  I  N  T  E  S  T  I  N  E  I  T
E  R  N  R  O  I  L  I  P  W  E  Ü  A  B  U  I
L  A  H  R  O  I  V  L  A  R  E  B  E  L  W  N
C  D  A  T  D  Y  E  E  E  R  O  H  B  S  E  I
S  K  N  B  F  E  E  B  R  L  B  C  T  G  A  H
U  C  G  N  N  W  N  N  U  V  D  A  A  R  G  O
M  I  G  N  D  Ü  N  N  D  A  R  M  I  Ü  O  S
L  D  A  S  F  F  G  M  R  I  H  O  E  O  S  E
T  Y  O  F  U  S  Z  T  S  O  K  T  E  Ü  W  I
H  I  M  U  S  K  E  L  N  A  R  S  V  E  E  R
I  Ü  U  G  U  R  Y  S  I  A  H  E  R  Z  G  E
I  G  E  H  I  R  N  N  E  M  N  Ü  D  H  N  T
Ü  E  C  E  R  E  C  H  V  E  O  T  V  D  U  R
H  E  N  I  T  S  E  T  N  I  E  G  R  A  L  A
D  L  E  A  W  X  I  D  N  E  P  P  A  M  O  O
```

APPENDIX	ANHANG
ARTERIES	ARTERIEN
BLOOD	BLUT
BRAIN	GEHIRN
HEART	HERZ
KIDNEY	NIERE
LARGE INTESTINE	DICKDARM
LIVER	LEBER
LUNGS	LUNGE
MUSCLES	MUSKELN
SMALL INTESTINE	DÜNNDARM
SPLEEN	MILZ
STOMACH	MAGEN
VEINS	VENEN

The Earth is an enormous place that time has divided up into continents and oceans. Take some time and memorize these words that define our Earth.

```
A F R I K A S E Ä R O T A U Q Ä
S N Ä E E O C L O P D Ü S A L G
I O E U A L N O D U W O K O A E
E R L R R S O T N O U I N K S U
N T Y O A O Ü P I T T G I R I R
E H I P C D T D H N I R L X T O
O A B A I S A A T E N A N K P
E M T Z T O M L U M U N E S R E
E E F I C E T D A Q E O T N A L
N R A F R A E D W T E R S Y T O
O I H I A F R I C A I R I O N P
R C C K T O O A O R L T A K A H
D A R G N E T I E R B L U H A T
P E G D A R G N E G N Ä L D T R
O A T L A N T I C O C E A N E O
L D F M P A C I F I C O C E A N
```

AFRICA	AFRIKA
ANTARCTICA	ANTARKTIS
ASIA	ASIEN
ATLANTIC OCEAN	ATLANTIK
CONTINENT	KONTINENT
EQUATOR	ÄQUATOR
EUROPE	EUROPA
LATITUDE	BREITENGRAD
LONGITUDE	LÄNGENGRAD
NORTH AMERICA	NORDAMERIKA
NORTH POLE	NORDPOL
PACIFIC OCEAN	PAZIFIK
SOUTH AMERICA	SÜDAMERIKA
SOUTH POLE	SÜDPOL

Time to zoom in and take a look at some geographical features that make up our planet. Fly over mountains, forests and glaciers as you reflect on the beauty of nature.

```
R F M D G P C P H E O A Z C E X
S F E E R A R O C ß T A Ü ß A
E I E S E E A N T I A E L ß L A
Y R R E H D T C A W L E N R G N
I N R R C L R A I E I I B I B S
E E I T S A F R R E Z E V V S O
R L ß T T W ß B E K R O C E A N
E L I E E U E I K D L D E R ß U
F A R C L R L E E C E R I O I A
F R R F G E O N A K L U V O H D
M O U N T A I N B T S A O C Ü S
A K R S L H O S S A T L L E S X
Ü C Ü E R A Ü T L E R Y S H M N
A W S M S E K A L A A Ü I H N I
E N ß C I T Y D Z N N I T I M S
I U M R K Ü S T E Y D D T T Ü L
```

BEACH	STRAND
CITY	STADT
COAST	KÜSTE
CORAL REEF	KORALLENRIFF
CRATER	KRATER
DESERT	WÜSTE
FOREST	WALD
GLACIER	GLETSCHER
ISLAND	INSEL
LAKE	SEE
MOUNTAIN	BERG
OCEAN	OZEAN
RIVER	FLUß
SEA	MEER
VOLCANO	VULKAN

Today's weather forecast shows a 100% chance of learning some important weather terms.

```
J A R S G W A R M N R O W D R E
O P N I I I I F W A R M C S E T
O T Y N D B N Ö I C R L L S S E
N T D Y H E E N H C S Ö F A H D
E I N D I D C U O N N E H X G E
G L I U L N R D A S U N A A R O
O I W O H R I K R C H G N B P O
B G C L I M I E H E I S S Z R C
N H K C U R D T F U L I N A E Z
E T A H R N W Z T I L B P T G E
G N O U U E Y O A K O T V A E Y
E I H H E H N G B W L E B E N T
R N T O V A N N O N H Ö E H U Ö
E G L N A E U N O F I E W E W U
S I A E A G S I D D N A R E Y U
E N K Q Y C I R T E M O R A B R
```

BAROMETRIC pressure	LUFTDRUCK
CLOUDY	BEWÖLKT
COLD	KALT
FOG	NEBEL
HOT	HEISS
HUMID	FEUCHT
HURRICANE	HURRIKAN
LIGHTNING	BLITZ
RAIN	REGEN
RAINBOW	REGENBOGEN
SNOW	SCHNEE
SUNNY	SONNIG
THUNDER	DONNER
WARM	WARM
WINDY	WINDIG

Let's go on a word safari to search for some of Africa's most famous animals. Elephants and lions are hiding somewhere below.

```
G O H T R A W B D T S ß A Q F E
G O R I L L A T N R U A E D Q B
H Ö R P C B I A E A A R B E Z I
I N D I O H F O R H S P I I A Ö
P D S O L E E T N Y K H E A ß U
P R N E L L S E I E D F O G O W
O E L E P H A N T N F S S R S U
P F E P O L I T N A C E D O N I
O P F Z E B R A R H H L R A E L
T L F O N P H I I C O E A N D F
A I A T Ä A G M I O C O P T E P
M N R H Y W P R N O E P O E I A
U Z I Z H A T M N D L A E L S V
S D G Y N S D I I Ö E R L O R I
Ö I M S O P H O W H K D Ä P H A
E S E W A R Z E N S C H W E I N
```

ANTELOPE	ANTILOPE
BABOON	PAVIAN
CHEETAH	GEPARD
CHIMPANZEE	SCHIMPANSE
ELEPHANT	ELEFANT
GIRAFFE	GIRAFFE
GORILLA	GORILLA
HIPPOPOTAMUS	NILPFERD
HYENA	HYÄNE
LEOPARD	LEOPARD
LION	LÖWE
OSTRICH	STRAUß
RHINOCEROS	NASHORN
WARTHOG	WARZENSCHWEIN
ZEBRA	ZEBRA

A recent study estimated that there are approximately 8.7 million different species of life on Earth. Below are just a few examples for you to learn.

```
P O L A R B E A R E E O E O G J
I N O R A U G A J R A W S R P N
N F G R K R J P U P E H W G O T
G L C M A U L T I E R S T O S F
U E E I P G Y D Z N E A U D L N
I D I M H N N T H G B L U O E F
N E W S A Ä A A T U T O W G M W
Q R P C B K T I K I N T M I A D
R M U L E Ä G T G N B D L E C J
Z A O F S E R E O A S B C B F L
E U I O R W R L T L E A A R R D
C S R X S H C U F T M O T R H R
B E U U A E L C H Q S N O A Ä Z
M L A S F O R N I T A S X T O W
P M E S V S T N Ä P M R U T H H
N T M S H S L C N A H T R A C L
```

BAT	FLEDERMAUS
CAMEL	KAMEL
CAT	KATZE
DOG	HUND
FOX	FUCHS
JAGUAR	JAGUAR
KANGAROO	KÄNGURU
MOOSE	ELCH
MOUSE	MAUS
MULE	MAULTIER
PENGUIN	PINGUIN
POLAR BEAR	EISBÄR
RABBIT	HASE
TIGER	TIGER
WOLF	WOLF

Another study estimates that approximatley 150-200 species are going extinct every 24 hours. Find the animals below before they disappear forever.

```
C E I C H H Ö R N C H E N E H H
N N I E W H C S L E H C A T S S
B E Ä L E S H S L N N M E I Q C
A J B I B E R I O A A S G O U H
C O Ö D R O D O F R M N N D I W
K L H O Ö O C R C L F A A E R A
E A P K C C O H R A T K L Ä R R
N M L O A G I R W Ä R E H L E Z
H A R R R P K R A E B K C A L B
Ö C T K M C N D I N J H S R E Ä
R R O U R T U T Ö E G E C A V R
N E N S G G K P O N D U V S R O
C K R L T N S N I A E E T T A R
H U M D I F A Ö N N R S U A E W
E U L T C R A R Ä O E O W L N E
N I S N A W I L O P N E X T E E
```

BEAVER	BIBER
BLACK BEAR	SCHWARZBÄR
CHIPMUNK	BACKENHÖRNCHEN
CROCODILE	KROKODIL
FROG	FROSCH
LLAMA	LAMA
ORANGUTAN	ORANG-UTAN
OWL	EULE
PORCUPINE	STACHELSCHWEIN
RACCOON	WASCHBÄR
RAT	RATTE
SKUNK	STINKTIER
SNAKE	SCHLANGE
SQUIRREL	EICHHÖRNCHEN

The blue whale is the largest animal on Earth. It's heart is the size of a car and can weigh as much as 50 elephants. Search the depths of the puzzle below for some other fascinating sea creatures.

```
E O A W Ö D J N H R Ö N K S T T
P A W S C H I L D K R Ö T E R E
M L A E S H U M M E R E M M U H
N M L E P S O C T O P U S U V E
L N U L S I G S E E H U N D T R
U Ö O Ö D F E E E L D C U S T S
T D L W R E T S B O L I S E W W
J T A E S S L O F B R A U I T H
E I W Ö H E Ö P E A A C U Q F A
L S T A R F I S H N T R A Q S L
L U R N L E O W L I H A K E ß E
Y K E S R R A H D Ö N B A G L T
F M W T Ö L O E E R S L I T O T
I B H G R H ß ß N N I S R N E S
S O C U A M A H C O ß U A I E ß
H C S I F N E T N I T O E R D H
```

TURTLE	SCHILDKRÖTE
CRAB	KRABBE
DOLPHIN	DELPHIN
FISH	FISCH
JELLYFISH	QUALLE
LOBSTER	HUMMER
OCTOPUS	HUMMER
ORCA	SCHWERTWAL
SEA LION	SEELÖWE
SEAL	SEEHUND
SHARK	HAI
SQUID	TINTENFISCH
STARFISH	SEESTERN
WALRUS	WALROß
WHALE	WAL

Are you married? Do you have any siblings?
Here is a list of terms that will help you to
describe your nearest and dearest

```
N E C H E L V E W H N I E C E S
E F R E D U R B R S I B E T W M
C K I N D E R F E W C T N E H U
T A T N H H A H E L H A H L H T
R E T T U M ß O R G T P L S F T
E E A A I F I N O G E E Q E L E
H F T L F P A R E N T S R H A R
T T Y A E E O M E R K S O N R E
O F R D V I ß B I T D E V H A T
M K A A S ß R T E L A L L F N S
D O B U U O O N O T I V I I E I
N ß T G T C E R E T S E W H C S
A ß S H H E K O G F T T A Y C A
R C E T E L C N U ß F U C A E C
G R E E L R T S O D N E Z D ß A
O R G R A N D F A T H E R T R O
```

AUNT	TANTE
BROTHER	BRUDER
CHILDREN	KINDER
DAUGHTER	TOCHTER
FAMILY	FAMILIE
FATHER	VATER
GRANDFATHER	GROßVATER
GRANDMOTHER	GROßMUTTER
MOTHER	MUTTER
NEPHEW	NEFFE
NIECE	NICHTE
PARENTS	ELTERN
SISTER	SCHWESTER
SON	SOHN
UNCLE	ONKEL

Here are some more family members that you might be particularly fond of (or perhaps not)

```
A S W A L N I R E T H G U A D R
S C H W A G E R E E L R I G J E
R H M O T H E R I N L A W N E T
S W G B R O T H E R I N L A W H
W I W R F U M S H N I D H S T C
A E W T A H A H S R N D W P E O
L G W A L N I R E H T A F I W T
N E I X L I D G F D Y U M N F R
I R D E F N Ä S J U N G E E X E
R V N D E W I W O E H H I W H G
E A A V H V G N N N C T S L G E
T T B C I L E K O D N E M E A I
S E S O B C E M Ä S H R E K E W
I R U D Y L Ä M I I N M W N E H
S C H W I E G E R M U T T E R C
S I S N H O S R E G E I W H C S
```

BROTHER-IN-LAW	SCHWAGER
BOY	JUNGE
DAUGHTER-IN-LAW	SCHWIEGERTOCHTER
FATHER-IN-LAW	SCHWIEGERVATER
GIRL	MÄDCHEN
GRANDDAUGHTER	ENKELIN
GRANDSON	ENKEL
HUSBAND	EHEMANN
MOTHER-IN-LAW	SCHWIEGERMUTTER
SISTER-IN-LAW	SCHWÄGERIN
SON-IN-LAW	SCHWIEGERSOHN
WIFE	FRAU

Actions speak louder than words. Here is a
list of common verbs that you might encounter
in your travels.

```
I  N  E  L  H  A  Z  E  B  Ö  T  D  N  R  R  M
N  L  E  Ö  N  Y  G  O  N  H  H  S  A  Ö  T  H
L  E  N  F  A  E  S  S  T  A  S  A  K  T  I  N
E  M  G  R  A  E  H  O  T  I  Z  S  I  S  A  E
S  A  E  A  H  L  R  C  N  O  E  N  L  G  W  G
H  E  T  E  R  E  H  G  O  M  N  J  D  C  O  A
C  G  N  K  A  F  E  C  C  K  P  F  O  P  T  R
E  N  F  D  N  N  S  T  S  K  N  I  H  T  O  T
W  A  R  T  E  N  E  O  G  N  I  S  O  T  F  T
T  H  N  G  S  F  I  S  H  A  D  C  L  X  O  L
N  C  L  E  S  E  N  E  E  R  O  U  L  A  L  T
T  O  S  L  E  E  P  E  T  O  G  E  S  H  L  E
F  T  O  C  A  R  R  Y  K  O  R  K  Ö  T  O  N
O  U  O  D  R  N  E  W  H  N  P  R  H  T  W  S
I  L  L  B  N  U  L  I  T  O  E  A  T  E  E  R
T  J  E  H  E  V  D  H  M  N  A  D  Y  E  T  G
```

TO ASK	FRAGEN
TO BE	SEIN
TO CARRY	TRAGEN
TO CHANGE	WECHSELN
TO COOK	KOCHEN
TO EAT	ESSEN
TO FOLLOW	FOLGEN
TO HEAR	HÖREN
TO PAY	BEZAHLEN
TO READ	LESEN
TO SEE	SEHEN
TO SING	SINGEN
TO SLEEP	SCHLAFEN
TO THINK	DENKEN
TO WAIT	WARTEN

VERBS 2

There are thousands of verbs in use today.
Here are some more popular verbs to practice.
Find the translations below.

```
E N E N E S S E I L H C S T N T
T D N A T S R E D N U O T E O Y
W H V E R S T E H E N M B T V A
A P T H F I E O C S T E A P B R
S A L G J U H M C C I K T K R B
S P R S N A A Z P L E H O T O E
U N R T B W O K A T O M E S F I
C K A E P S O T R I M S O S K T
H R N E C R E I S E N E E C O E
E O D O T H N S N G V N U T O N
N W L V K K E E I A R I R O L T
E O L W E V F N H X T A E D O O
D T E N O L Y O T M V S E R T F
N D S L E O T O O E E V O I R I
I G O H A E L V L I E N N N N N
F T T E G N M A E S E L I K V D
```

TO CLOSE	SCHLIESSEN
TO COME	KOMMEN
TO DO	TUN
TO DRINK	TRINKEN
TO FIND	FINDEN
TO HAVE	HABEN
TO HELP	HELFEN
TO LOOK FOR	ETWAS SUCHEN
TO LOVE	LIEBEN
TO SELL	VERKAUFEN
TO SPEAK	SPRECHEN
TO TAKE	NEHMEN
TO TRAVEL	REISEN
TO UNDERSTAND	VERSTEHEN
TO WORK	ARBEITEN

Languages typically have a mix of regular and irregular verbs. A regular verb has a predictable conjugation. An irregular verb has a conjugation that does not follow the typical pattern. In English, many of the most common verbs are irregular.

```
N I E S E G A L R E D N I O Ö L
N E D L U H C S W D E E U T D S
E J B G A N T O T S V S T R Y Ö
P C H I E N O O S N E S T D O R
O N R H E T W A K P A I O Ö W T
O C E E Y R L W G N I W G I O A
T G N B I R H O G T O E O T L E
O E N T E T N C R O H W L T L H
B T E V T G E N S T T W H E E Z
E Z N L H C N M O O O J H S N Ö
A Y T L N N R L W G B P E H F A
B Y A A E E E A N I U F L F G G
L S D O E A L F H V Y E N A E X
E O A A V K A A U E L E A H Y Ö
T O L E A R N T T A N Z E N O E
O L W H A P S H T H K N C D C Q
```

TO BE ABLE TO	IN DER LAGE SEIN
TO BUY	KAUFEN
TO DANCE	TANZEN
TO GIVE	GEBEN
TO GO	GEHEN
TO KNOW	WISSEN
TO LEARN	LERNEN
TO LEAVE	VERLASSEN
TO OPEN	ÖFFNEN
TO OWE	SCHULDEN
TO PLAY	SPIELEN
TO RUN	RENNEN
TO WALK	GEHEN
TO WANT	WOLLEN
TO WRITE	SCHREIBEN

One of the greatures pleasures of travelling to another country is sampling the local cuisine. Study the word list below so you can order with confidence.

```
D R B K D U C L A T H D L N A H
R D L C T C T H E E S S F A D A
M I L C H T B X B H F R U I T T
M G R E T A W U E R Ü D Ü G X H
Ä H E I A N T L T C H T A L A S
S S T Ä P T L Q H T R U O L F R
E U D A E G H T B R E A D L E I
L D S R E T E I G W A R E N D Ä
B T Ä M E M M W T M T I T S E Ä
A L Ü C I S T R S H S S A Q Ä T
T S H S E Z S F A C A Y L O N K
E O G T R U P A H N L M O W R E
G G R T E C L S W S A E C I R H
E P A B I K N J D N D N O E L Y
V I R O S E D A L O K O H C S N
O Ü N R W R A A N R H E C I A E
```

BREAD	BROT
BUTTER	BUTTER
CHEESE	KÄSE
CHOCOLATE	SCHOKOLADE
EGGS	EIER
FLOUR	MEHL
FRUIT	FRÜCHTE
MEAT	FLEISCH
MILK	MILCH
PASTA	TEIGWAREN
RICE	REIS
SALAD	SALAT
SUGAR	ZUCKER
VEGETABLES	GEMÜSE
WATER	WASSER

Want more? You have quite an appetite (for learning). Feast on this delicious buffet of mouth watering words.

```
L Z W L H M R E V T D E I O I S
H H L I M R N H F D I W D N G L
C E T A R A D T L O A A T R T X
S C L G S C S B T L O H U E L E
I O A H I F I E Q D E U V P T O
E O S K E N S R V H E L J P W M
L E S E E I O Y N K E M O E I A
F O B K I O S H O N E Y G P P E
E O A S U P P E X G S R H F I R
N V N E H C U K R E U Ä U E D C
I K D I A A Ö V E D H R R F T E
E W R K O R R I T N H E T F O C
W L I O O H R W C H I C K E N I
H D N O P E E H R B L W R R K A
C E H C S I E L F D N I R F Ö Z
S O U P N N B M A L Ö Z M P L N
```

BEEF	RINDFLEISCH
BEER	BIER
CAKE	KUCHEN
CHICKEN	HÄHNCHEN
COOKIES	KEKSE
HONEY	HONIG
ICE CREAM	EIS
LAMB	LAMM
OIL	ÖL
PEPPER	PFEFFER
PORK	SCHWEINEFLEISCH
SALT	SALZ
SOUP	SUPPE
WINE	WEIN
YOGURT	JOGHURT

A fruit is the part of a plant that surrounds the seeds, whereas a vegetable is a plant that has some other edible part. Tomatoes, cucumbers and peppers are three examples of fruit that are often classified as vegetables.

```
M N E R E E B L E D I E H E P N
E O S E E G R A N A T A P F E L
F S O N R R P N M A T I L B N S
I H K O S D O L N B N A U O O E
T C I L A L B A U E U A L R L I
H I R E E A R E A M R E A A E R
T S P M N G U P E T M E C N M R
G R A P E S P B N R P E Z G R E
E I R M T L A I E L E G I E E B
T F O H E N E T X R E N T B S W
H P T A A W A A F H G M R I S A
O S W N T W F L T V C I O R A R
I I A T O C I R P A A A N N W T
D S S T A I M Y Y G M B E E E S
O H S C O O O R A N G E N P I S
K L H E S E I R R E B E U L B U
```

APRICOT	APRIKOSE
BLUEBERRIES	HEIDELBEEREN
EGGPLANT	AUBERGINE
GRAPES	WEINTRAUBEN
LEMON	ZITRONE
MELON	MELONE
ORANGE	ORANGE
PEACH	PFIRSICH
PEAR	BIRNE
PINEAPPLE	ANANAS
PLUM	PFLAUME
POMEGRANATE	GRANATAPFEL
STRAWBERRIES	ERDBEEREN
WATERMELON	WASSERMELONE

There are more than 7000 different varieties of apples being grown around the world today. Check out our produce section below for some more fresh and tasty fruit.

```
R E P P E P N E E R G F H H O R
H O N I G M E L O N E T C Y E J
B C T H C H E R R I E S E D Q A
I L G E I S A P F E L L P E G O
N E A R R M N R U A L E M E L H
I Z B C Ü P B R I O P I L B A E
H U R A K N A E W P L B H A O H
C C O P N B E P E R E A Ü N T O
C C M P H A E R R R I E T A O N
U H B L T P N R P I E C I N M E
Z I E E P D U A R A K N Y E A H
E N E E E E P M T I P A F G T C
U I R G O R A S P B E R R I E S
T O E S I B R Ü K K A S I E G R
K D N K T E T T E M I L R K C I
O T A M O T F E Q F G N I Q A K
```

APPLE	APFEL
BANANA	BANANE
BLACKBERRIES	BROMBEEREN
CANTALOUPE	HONIGMELONE
CHERRIES	KIRSCHEN
FIG	FEIGE
GREEN PEPPER	GRÜNER PAPRIKA
LIME	LIMETTE
PUMPKIN	KÜRBIS
RASPBERRIES	HIMBEEREN
RED PEPPER	ROTER PAPRIKA
TOMATO	TOMATE
YELLOW PEPPER	GELBER PAPRIKA
ZUCCHINI	ZUCCHINI

VEGETABLES 1

A 2013 study estimated that up to 87% of people in the United States do no consume their daily recommended portion of vegetables. Here is a list of vegetables that you should probably be eating more of.

```
L A H L H O K N E M U L B X L S
F E R E A R T I S C H O C K E T
N L Ü F T E E E E T B E N G B Ü
F L B U E T O K A L E O K R E I
H E E R O T O S U P B E Ü Ü I T
Ü G N T A P P R U L Y L B N W S
R R E T T I A M A G T T Ü K Z S
E A O K N U O U E K A G A O T E
I P U A O N C I I N A R C H A G
L S C K O H L E I R T N A L L A
O H T D H O C P L O E P R P A B
C O E E C E S I F E L O R L S B
C J I C D H C F T O N I O N C A
O R O D H C E L E R Y K T C E C
R R E W O L F I L U A C H E P E
B S T A N G E N S E L L E R I E
```

ARTICHOKE	ARTISCHOCKE
ASPARAGUS	SPARGEL
BEETS	RÜBEN
BROCCOLI	BROCCOLI
CABBAGE	KOHL
CARROT	KAROTTE
CAULIFLOWER	BLUMENKOHL
CELERY	STANGENSELLERIE
GARLIC	KNOBLAUCH
KALE	GRÜNKOHL
LETTUCE	SALAT
ONION	ZWIEBEL
POTATOES	KARTOFFELN
SPINACH	SPINAT

There's no place like home. Below is a list of words that are related to house and home.

```
E  Ü  U  E  G  I  Z  N  N  W  N  D  E  B  O  M
J  F  M  Z  U  F  A  R  H  T  S  W  E  G  O  D
Ü  O  E  O  U  T  U  P  N  S  O  T  A  O  W  I
S  O  P  N  O  I  N  E  A  H  T  A  R  L  O  N
C  R  S  G  C  R  M  N  N  R  C  H  S  I  H  I
H  L  F  A  F  E  D  Z  K  I  T  C  H  E  N  N
L  V  O  R  S  A  I  E  I  A  T  M  S  T  U  G
A  S  S  A  M  M  Ü  A  B  M  B  H  E  Y  N  R
F  W  B  G  M  S  I  U  V  V  Ü  N  A  N  G  O
Z  I  R  E  M  M  I  Z  S  S  E  W  O  U  T  O
I  N  R  G  L  F  E  N  S  T  E  R  C  S  S  M
M  D  Q  A  E  A  H  Ü  A  V  E  H  A  I  O  I
M  O  O  R  G  N  I  V  I  L  N  S  C  S  O  S
E  W  D  A  C  H  I  R  L  E  I  A  U  Ü  E  H
R  C  A  G  E  Y  D  E  E  C  Z  O  E  O  K  N
O  H  A  A  E  M  K  X  D  A  U  T  C  N  H  O
```

APARTMENT	WOHNUNG
BASEMENT	KELLER
BATHROOM	WC
BED	BETT
BEDROOM	SCHLAFZIMMER
DINING ROOM	ESSZIMMER
DRIVEWAY	ZUFARHTSWEG
FENCE	ZAUN
GARAGE	GARAGE
HOUSE	HAUS
KITCHEN	KÜCHE
LAWN	RASEN
LIVING ROOM	WOHNZIMMER
ROOF	DACH
WINDOW	FENSTER

It is estimated that one tenth of all furniture purchased in Britain comes from IKEA. Perhaps you have assembled a few of these items yourself.

```
T E E E O F O I E U I H I V C O
A R I K I C T E L R A E F L N T
B O E M V A C U U M O I A N O W
L D T P D R E S S E R M I E B A
E R T E P P I C H E P T I U K S
R Y E I S E U Q P G A M T F R H
T E L I O T B L N E T H A I O I
D R I H D H A A Ä W T U A L N N
M O O L K C H U D A C T H A L G
M C T A E R F O B E S E I S E M
K O M M O D E O T S W U C S U A
M I N V Z C N H A A A A T F C C
N W I C U R T A I N S U N Ä H H
W A S S E R H A H N E S G N T I
E N I H C S A M H C S A W E E N
G W Ä S C H E T R O C K N E R E
```

BATHTUB	BADEWANNE
CARPET	TEPPICH
CHANDELIER	KRONLEUCHTER
CURTAIN	VORHANG
DRESSER	KOMMODE
DRYER	WÄSCHETROCKNER
FAUCET	WASSERHAHN
FIREPLACE	KAMIN
LAMP	LAMPE
STAIRS	TREPPE
TABLE	TISCH
TOILET	TOILETTE
VACUUM	STAUBSAUGER
WASHING MACHINE	WASCHMASCHINE

Here is a list of some more common household items and modern conveniences. Search the grid for the words listed below

```
D L N F L U R T O C K K N I S T
S E Ü E Ü A H E E O Ü I S L P M
R R C A K A T I H H F C S E E G
I E G K L C L O L S H E H S E I
A A F L E I E S W R A C N S E B
H N W R N N C B E S S W C E I N
C A I G I H V I H U L H H S V G
Y A F E R G B E D C I T T S I O
E A M A T T E E N R S N R T I C
N D N A I S S R R T T A T O T D
M K D S T K N S A T I E W S A M
I T C T Ü R P R D T R L H T E I
H H E G F Ü A N O B O O A D L R
C W O L L I P T E H W R A T I R
L E G E I P S T Z E C F N I O O
B I R C M A T T R E S S G A L R
```

CHAIR	SESSEL
CEILING FAN	DECKENVENTILATOR
CHIMNEY	SCHORNSTEIN
CRIB	GITTERBETT
DESK	SCHREIBTISCH
DISHWASHER	GESCHIRRSPÜLER
HALLWAY	FLUR
MATTRESS	MATRATZE
MIRROR	SPIEGEL
OVEN	OFEN
PILLOW	KISSEN
REFRIGERATOR	KÜHLSCHRANK
SHOWER	DUSCHE
SINK	WASCHBECKEN

Table setting etiquette dictates that the forks be placed on the left hand side of the plate and knives on the right. Here are some items that you might find on your table, probably in the wrong location.

```
H T L T N O F T T R R W E L S M
V D T K O H T O L C E L B A T M
D E G U M E E Ö R I H P Ü N I T
N P L A T E F I N K C A P M Ö L
L A A U Z F T G E R T E B E E A
I E S T E L L E R E I N O O P S
R R B L P A A W S F P D W O T T
K U E E S A H S Y F L Ö L E I A
S R G B C H W I N E G L A S S B
H T U A H H O M F F D S C S R L
T I T G Ü E E F S P P H A L E E
N I H T S S Ö R E O D L E Ö T S
E Ü O E S L U U O E G H E F A P
S A O E E E D N C U A T S F C O
O A R E L N I K P A N D I E Q O
F I T E T T E I V R E S T L S N
```

BOWL	SCHÜSSEL
FORK	GABEL
GLASS	GLAS
KNIFE	MESSER
MUG	BECHER
NAPKIN	SERVIETTE
PEPPER	PFEFFER
PITCHER	KRUG
PLATE	TELLER
SALT	SALZ
SPOON	LÖFFEL
TABLECLOTH	TISCHDECKE
TABLESPOON	ESSLÖFFEL
TEASPOON	TEELÖFFEL
WINE GLASS	WEINGLAS

Time to get out the tool box and do some repairs on our vocabulary. Try to hammer a few of these words and their translations into you brain.

```
U N T E R L E G S C H E I B E S
S B O L T S B S T I Ä T T N R R
C E O W E R C S C M N R A E E E
H N M H S H L M E H E W V M H I
R E E Ä R E O S E D R I M S E L
A Ä G A G E S E D E R A O R I P
U E U A A B R A N D H I U T Z J
B B N H A B L C W E Y S L B N B
E N H N A W H E A S A L U L E H
N R D A S M R T S E V E I G B O
M U G I Q C M E M S N V W A U N
U H T L S Ü Z E S Ä Ü E A A A Ü
T L I C N E P R R S W L S R R O
T Ü D C E A N E G N A Z H H H V
E T F I T S I E L B A W E C C L
R Ä S Q H Ü G L E I T E R G S A
```

BOLT	SCHRAUBE
DRILL	BOHRER
HAMMER	HAMMER
LADDER	LEITER
LEVEL	WASSERWAAGE
NAIL	NAGEL
NUT	SCHRAUBENMUTTER
PENCIL	BLEISTIFT
PLIERS	ZANGEN
SAW	SÄGE
SCREW	SCHRAUBE
SCREWDRIVER	SCHRAUBENZIEHER
TAPE MEASURE	MESSBAND
WASHER	UNTERLEGSCHEIBE
WRENCH	SCHLÜSSEL

Globally there are 1.2 billion pairs of jeans sold annually. That is a lot of denim! Take a look at this list of other common articles of clothing.

```
C E I E T R W E P S P P A Y V O
T O S C H L A F A N Z U G G E P
M O A T O A E T S E W L W V H F
H H M D R Ü T W W Ü O L Ü K U T
N H A T R O E S N V E O I U H O
B B J T A A H Q E T H V Y Ü C S
A A A N T S L S N V U E H C S O
T D P E E S C A R F H R Q E D N
H E R C S K M T H O C T R M N G
R M T K T N C T A C S D L Z A E
O A Ü T N L E O O I S T R O H S
B N L I A E E A S J Ü O M U F R
E T X E P W T B A H U T C C S A
L E T R Ü G A D E F O N Y K E A
F L M T T H M R O D I E L K S G
T Ü H N H Ü I W K E E C S I F A
```

BATHROBE	BADEMANTEL
BELT	GÜRTEL
COAT	MANTEL
DRESS	KLEID
GLOVES	HANDSCHUHE
HAT	HUT
NECKTIE	KRAWATTE
PAJAMAS	SCHLAFANZUG
PANTS	HOSE
SCARF	SCHAL
SHOES	SCHUHE
SHORTS	SHORTS
SOCKS	SOCKEN
SWEATER	PULLOVER
VEST	WESTE

More than 2 billion t-shirts are sold each year! How many of these other items can be found in your closet?

```
R  U  I  V  G  U  B  S  N  A  E  J  H  K  R  L
K  L  E  I  D  U  N  G  K  P  R  B  C  L  H  P
C  E  S  E  F  N  Z  D  D  I  O  O  R  E  O  M
E  C  A  L  K  C  E  N  E  O  R  W  H  F  S  T
T  I  U  S  M  I  W  S  A  R  D  T  U  E  O  H
R  L  G  U  Z  N  A  U  P  E  W  I  D  I  C  O
I  B  R  B  L  N  A  S  V  E  D  E  N  T  L  S
H  Q  R  R  D  N  E  P  G  E  N  A  A  S  O  E
S  L  H  A  L  S  K  E  T  T  E  W  B  R  T  N
O  I  L  C  N  O  I  N  O  H  T  D  M  B  H  T
H  E  N  E  R  L  S  D  Q  S  E  W  R  O  I  R
N  T  J  L  F  U  V  E  I  P  L  M  A  O  N  Ä
B  X  M  E  I  R  A  R  M  B  A  N  D  T  G  G
G  A  X  T  A  E  W  S  L  A  D  N  A  S  D  E
I  L  E  E  U  N  T  E  R  W  Ä  S  C  H  E  R
H  I  O  C  Z  R  S  F  E  W  P  E  N  M  K  L
```

WRIST WATCH	ARMBANDUHR
BOOTS	STIEFEL
BOW TIE	FLIEGE
BRA	BH
BRACELET	ARMBAND
CLOTHING	KLEIDUNG
JEANS	JEANS
NECKLACE	HALSKETTE
SANDALS	SANDALEN
SHIRT	HEMD
SKIRT	ROCK
SUIT	ANZUG
SUSPENDERS	HOSENTRÄGER
SWIM SUIT	BADEANZUG
UNDERWEAR	UNTERWÄSCHE

The majority of people take less than half an hour to get ready in the morning. Some can be ready in less than 5 minutes, whereas some take over an hour. Here is a list of things that might be a part of your morning routine.

```
C I N D A T O E D I E S N H A Z
O T E R E N O I T I D N O C Ö T
N A M E A O N O B N A Y L E R N
T R E S A Z D M T E F I E S S M
A A T S Y T O O T H P A S T E M
C P N A S C S R R S B L T Z M H
T P A W S W S A T A I R A O A A
L A R D O N E I P P N H U A H I
E R O N L G C T P N N T R S N R
N E D U F K S E T B H S E L H D
S I O M L H N O Ü W P A E H K R
E S E O A S F R A Ü T W Z Ö A Y
S A D M T Ö S S L P E R F U M E
M R P I N T H U C P A R F Ü M R
S O F N E S N I L T K A T N O K
O T C O D G P O O P M A H S T A
```

COMB	KAMM
CONDITIONER	HAARSPÜLUNG
CONTACT LENSES	KONTAKTLINSEN
DENTAL FLOSS	ZAHNSEIDE
DEODORANT	DEODORANT
HAIR DRYER	FÖN
LIPSTICK	LIPPENSTIFT
MOUTHWASH	MUNDWASSER
PERFUME	PARFÜM
RAZOR	RASIERAPPARAT
SHAMPOO	SHAMPOO
SOAP	SEIFE
TOOTHBRUSH	ZAHNBÜRSTE
TOOTHPASTE	ZAHNPASTA

Places to go and people to see. Here are some places that you might visit around town.

```
H F E U E R W A C H E N I E L U
K I C M U S E U M E E E M M E M
D R E K C Ü R B E C C F R U I E
E E A R A B A G K I N A U I S G
E S P N Ü U D Ü F F O H T D U T
F T U A K I F F O F I G T A P F
M A I P R E O H F O D U H T E E
U T R B E T N E A E A L C S R R
E I C M S R M H L U T F U L M H
S O J O E N M E A U S O E T A A
U N P U M P T A N U H O L M R U
M Q A A I R P O R T S C Q A K T
B B A H N H O F H K T Y S T T M
A Ü T S I C Z G W Ü E S E S V J
R T R T R A I N S T A T I O N D
S C H O O L A T I P S O H P N A
```

AIRPORT	FLUGHAFEN
BAR	BAR
BRIDGE	BRÜCKE
DEPARTMENT store	KAUFHAUS
FARM	BAUERNHOF
FIRE STATION	FEUERWACHE
HOSPITAL	KRANKENHAUS
LIGHTHOUSE	LEUCHTTURM
MUSEUM	MUSEUM
OFFICE	BÜRO
POST OFFICE	POSTAMT
SCHOOL	SCHULE
STADIUM	STADION
SUPERMARKET	SUPERMARKT
TRAIN STATION	BAHNHOF

The weekend is finally here. Where to you
feel like going tonight? Here are some more
places you can visit.

```
Ä É A D A P A R K A U A S H E O
F L E T O H K C E É K N A B V E
T R K Y A H R E S T A U R A N T
H N I R T E T D H H A F E N P C
B É B E A I E N N T A E C K O O
U O F T D P S O A P O E H F L L
R P S A O H U R O R M I F T I G
G Y U E C S O T E E U E L B Z G
Q C A H E C H F T V E A R B E A
C A H T P E A A S S I A T S I N
E M N I K C R S H A R N C S R B
W R R E N Y E O T Y T H U R E N
B A E R M I P I É L Ä A O Ä V R
R H P E E R O T S F E O S T I N
N P O L I C E S T A T I O N E R
S U N I V E R S I T Ä T O E R L
```

BANK	BANK
CASTLE	BURG
CEMETARY	FRIEDHOF
COFFEE SHOP	CAFÉ
HARBOR	HAFEN
HOTEL	HOTEL
LIBRARY	BIBLIOTHEK
OPERA HOUSE	OPERNHAUS
PARK	PARK
PHARMACY	APOTHEKE
POLICE STATION	POLIZEIREVIER
RESTAURANT	RESTAURANT
STORE	GESCHÄFT
THEATER	THEATER
UNIVERSITY	UNIVERSITÄT

Road trip time! Hop in your car, turn up the music and hit the open road. Make sure you study this list of road worthy translations before heading out.

```
B E N Z I N W E T T S H T E H O
O S A E T H G I L C I F F A R T
E S U H P Z T A L P K R A P H M
E A T B L O N E S G E R M H E S
R R O O E E T G A S R O E T K T
U T M F P M P S W R T R O N R O
T S O V M P O A S O O A H E E P
A N B C A L S T R U G A T D V S
N H I N I N I C O K B T D I O I
K A L N O F Y T H R I N O C O G
S B E I R C F U H I R N G C T N
T N H B L H N A C N L A G A U E
E I I E C F F I R I B D D L A G
L E S S A R T S M T E E J I O B
L T S L O N E W A Y S T R E E T
E L L E T S E T L A H S U B U S
```

AUTOMOBILE	AUTO
ACCIDENT	UNFALL
BUS	BUS
BUS STOP	BUSHALTESTELLE
GAS STATION	TANKSTELLE
GASOLINE	BENZIN
LANE	FAHRBAHN
MOTORCYCLE	MOTORRAD
ONE-WAY STREET	EINBAHNSTRASSE
PARKING LOT	PARKPLATZ
ROAD	STRASSE
STOP SIGN	STOPPSCHILD
TRAFFIC LIGHT	AMPEL
TRAFFIC	VERKEHR

There are many interesting ways of getting from A to B. Which mode of transportation will you choose?

```
E R E T T U N G S W A G E N H J
G U E Z R H A F I E Z I L O P T
U L C U B A T F T O H S S Y D F
E Ö N E N I R A M B U S A T Ä G
Z S A Ö T T N F E W F W O H O S
G C L O E K E I S Ö B O R T E Z
U H U B S C H R A U B E R R T S
L F B O R N K E S A B E C A Ä K
F A M Y L Ä O T I E T L O I A E
A H A P F E R R Y P E B U N M J
H R X T K M P U O P I B U H A Ä
R Z U P O L I C E C A R O O C C
R E G E A N I K A H D N H O C S
A U A N V L P U N N G U Z E T W
D G E L E L C Y C I B X I E L E
I S C H O O L B U S I E Ö E R M
```

AIRPLANE — FLUGZEUG
AMBULANCE — RETTUNGSWAGEN
BICYCLE — FAHRRAD
BOAT — BOOT
CANOE — KANU
FERRY — FÄHRE
FIRE TRUCK — LÖSCHFAHRZEUG
HELICOPTER — HUBSCHRAUBER
POLICE CAR — POLIZEIFAHRZEUG
SCHOOL BUS — SCHULBUS
SUBMARINE — UNTERSEEBOOT
SUBWAY — U-BAHN
TANK — PANZER
TRAIN — ZUG

Here are some popular languages from around the world. Maybe you already know one or two of them.

```
H C S I B A R A Ä Ä U I E M P A
C P O R T U G U E S E E T D O G
S Ä K H K O N O S N R H Q E R I
I Ö E E O K G Ä I S C O I U T H
S F E B R E O R A S I E C T U E
Ö H R R E H A R I H E S S S G Ö
Z P G E A D A N E E P T C C I T
N O E W N B A B S A C Ä A H E P
A L R A I P R E N P N H N N S O
R N M C A Ä N I N A A I I Ä I L
F I A J I A S Y I G F N S S S I
K S N S P H M L I T L R I C C S
H C C A D M A N D A R I N S H H
I H J B L T N E N G L I S H C T
R U S S I A N F Ä F R E N C H H
Ö K H C S I N E I L A T I A H S
```

ARABIC	ARABISCH
ENGLISH	ENGLISCH
FRENCH	FRANZÖSISCH
GERMAN	DEUTSCH
GREEK	GRIECHISCH
ITALIAN	ITALIENISCH
JAPANESE	JAPANISCH
KOREAN	KOREANISCH
MANDARIN	MANDARIN
POLISH	POLNISCH
PORTUGUESE	PORTUGIESISCH
RUSSIAN	RUSSISCH
SPANISH	SPANISCH
HEBREW	HEBRÄISCH

Statistics suggest that the average person may change careers 5-7 times in their lives.
Thinking about a change? Why not try one of these great professions?

```
D I U R F S E R A W F E H C Y T
R E T S E W H C S N E K N A R K
E T T Y U L T T E A C H E R P D
Y N A A E O L R E E O Z J P O I
W R R A R L R E L N I D A E L N
A E C E W D E E T M Y A F N I N
L E H N E A K H M S I I U T C A
Z N I N H T W E R I R R M E E S
A I T H R A R U K E S A T R O A
H G E I M M E O F E R H D O F O
N N K N A I C I R T C E L E F E
A E T N N H G W O N N T O L I P
R T N E N H I L O T L U T E C T
Z U G Q T S I Z I L O P J Z E S
T N I E L P E S V D O C T O R U
I A R C H I T E C T L A W N A A
```

ACTOR	DARSTELLER
ARCHITECT	ARCHITEKT
CARPENTER	ZIMMERMANN
CHEF	KOCH
DENTIST	ZAHNARZT
DOCTOR	ARZT
ELECTRICIAN	ELEKTRIKER
ENGINEER	INGENIEUR
FIRE FIGHTER	FEUERWEHRMANN
LAWYER	ANWALT
NURSE	KRANKENSCHWESTER
PILOT	PILOT
POLICE OFFICER	POLIZIST
TEACHER	LEHRER

What did you want to be when you were growing up? Was it one of these professions?

```
B R R O O E E R O M A C P A T T
U O E P A R A M E D I C N S N S
C L N C Z E E C R D B A I U A I
H I P E N A H E V A I T R N T R
H A M B O A K L R C R E I A N O
A T E P N I D B I A B T N T U L
L G L I T H I S U R Ä H O H O F
T O K I H E U R A T E V M L C D
E E L S R M S B E U C E T E C S
R O S S E F O R P L C H Ü T A R
P R O F E S S O R H T O E E D E
M U S I K E R O A B T R O R F Z
A D R E L T S N Ü K O E O D I N
Z N F L O R I S T O H W B P O Ä
P L N A I C I T I L O P R E S T
L D A M E T Z G E R E B M U L P
```

ACCOUNTANT	BUCHHALTER
ARTIST	KÜNSTLER
ATHLETE	SPORTLER
BARBER	BARBIER
BUTCHER	METZGER
DANCER	TÄNZER
FLORIST	FLORIST
MECHANIC	MECHANIKER
MUSICIAN	MUSIKER
PARAMEDIC	SANITÄTER
PLUMBER	KLEMPNER
POLITICIAN	POLITIKER
PROFESSOR	PROFESSOR
TAILOR	SCHNEIDER

There are thousands of unique and challenging careers out there to choose from. See if you can locate the following careers in the grid below.

```
F  L  I  G  H  T  A  T  T  E  N  D  A  N  T  F
A  H  P  O  N  Ü  U  R  E  I  D  L  O  S  N  L
R  E  Ü  O  T  N  T  Z  R  A  R  E  I  T  A  U
M  I  T  E  S  W  I  H  L  T  T  C  Ü  C  I  G
E  D  T  R  O  T  A  L  S  N  A  R  T  R  R  B
R  R  T  S  I  Ü  B  I  E  M  X  R  S  E  A  E
E  E  T  R  D  W  L  O  R  A  I  E  I  Z  N  G
I  K  N  Y  E  A  D  A  T  A  D  R  L  T  I  L
L  E  H  E  N  H  H  N  N  E  R  H  A  E  R  E
E  H  Z  R  D  P  C  R  A  A  I  A  N  S  E  I
W  T  U  T  Q  R  T  S  C  L  V  F  R  R  T  T
U  O  V  E  N  F  A  L  I  M  E  I  U  E  E  E
J  P  M  C  A  H  I  G  T  F  R  X  O  B  V  R
L  A  U  T  T  A  D  L  O  S  E  A  J  Ü  E  E
T  R  N  A  M  R  E  H  S  I  F  T  M  H  H  F
R  E  N  T  R  Ä  G  R  L  J  E  W  E  L  E  R
```

FARMER	LANDWIRT
FISHERMAN	FISCHER
FLIGHT ATTENDANT	FLUGBEGLEITER
GARDENER	GÄRTNER
JEWELER	JUWELIER
JOURNALIST	JOURNALIST
MAIL CARRIER	POSTBOTE
PHARMACIST	APOTHEKER
SOLDIER	SOLDAT
TAXI DRIVER	TAXIFAHRER
TRANSLATOR	ÜBERSETZER
VETERINARIAN	TIERARZT

SOLAR SYSTEM

In 2015, the New Horizons spacecraft successfully completed the first flyby of dwarf planet Pluto. There is still so much to see and explore in our own solar system. Here are some key words from our celestial backyard.

```
R C I S U N E V I K S S I V T T
A R J I U F E M S O C X S E O E
S A A T E A D O N M I I H N T N
O T P L R R R N S E T N O T M E
N E P T U N E D S T I D T G A I
N R H E S U P T R J U H N E D D
E R D W R L S W A M U W E E N E
N V U A U I E O M R E P S R A M
S M N T S M J T R S K R I F S O
Y U O H A H C U Q H E T C T T E
S T O N U S K O P S E S N U E T
T G M I O R N B M I W O L I R R
E S U N E V E C L E T P H S O Y
M C E M N R U T A S T E R O I D
O C E Z F O N I S U N A R U D I
E O F T N M E T S Y S R A L O S
```

SOLAR SYSTEM	SONNENSYSTEM
MERCURY	MERKUR
VENUS	VENUS
EARTH	ERDE
MOON	MOND
MARS	MARS
JUPITER	JUPITER
SATURN	SATURN
URANUS	URANUS
NEPTUNE	NEPTUN
PLUTO	PLUTO
SUN	SONNE
CRATER	KRATER
ASTEROID	ASTEROID
COMET	KOMET

Here are some musical instruments to get your foot tapping and your hands clapping.

```
T R U M P E T U L F L Ö T E Ü T
E H A R F E N R A E R R A T I G
B T A T E B T U O Ö I J R V R A
L A E R I M T A A M S O G I N K
A M G P P U K B M S M C E O O I
A B D P M Ö G U D B O E H L I N
H O E U I O D T O U U P L I D O
A U T U D P R N R C O R V N R M
R R M H W E E T W X E S I V O R
M I Ö Ü T N L S A S Y L O N C A
O N P Ö I E A S L E G Ü L F C H
N E N O H P O X A S Ü R I O A D
I T N Ü A C Ö Z L C T N N T R N
C E L L O V I T D I K A E U D U
A K K O R D E O N T I E M B R M
A T W R H D S G P P M S M A R T
```

ACCORDION	AKKORDEON
BAGPIPES	DUDELSACK
CELLO	CELLO
DRUMS	TROMMELN
FLUTE	FLÖTE
GUITAR	GITARRE
HARMONICA	MUNDHARMONIKA
HARP	HARFE
PIANO	FLÜGEL
SAXOPHONE	SAXOPHON
TAMBOURINE	TAMBURIN
TROMBONE	POSAUNE
TRUMPET	TROMPETE
TUBA	TUBA
VIOLIN	VIOLINE

This puzzle might make you happy, angry, or maybe even a little confused. See if you can complete this very emotional puzzle by finding all of the words in the grid.

```
A T S S U W E B T S B L E S C O
G Ö L R A D N G G C X R H U E O
W L S I L N E S H R S M W R S O
S C Ü B E R R A S C H T O P S U
E P L C E W P E H C G K R R E R
N R P G K P G R T R A U R I G T
S O F W Y L O N O H R R I S N R
E U H Ü S C I S A N C O E E E R
A D X T K O E C H L O Ü D D R I
R L O E N B O B H Y E I H T V W
Y L N N X N O E Ü H F G T C Ö R
Z E H D F R Y R G N A Ü O O S E
V Ü P U E O O N O I T O M E M V
K Ö S D E T I C X E O I O O K E
V E R L E G E N E R V O U S N H
D E M B A R R A S S E D A S T A
```

EMOTION	EMOTION
HAPPY	GLÜCKLICH
SAD	TRAURIG
EXCITED	AUFGEREGT
BORED	GELANGWEILT
SURPRISED	ÜBERRASCHT
SCARED	ERSCHROCKEN
ANGRY	WÜTEND
CONFUSED	VERWIRRT
WORRIED	BESORGT
NERVOUS	NERVÖS
PROUD	STOLZ
CONFIDENT	SELBSTBEWUSST
EMBARRASSED	VERLEGEN
SHY	SCHÜCHTERN

If you are feeling any symptoms of the
following conditions it might be time to visit
the doctor. When you are feeling better the
words below are waiting to be found.

```
N S N E T U L B N E S A N F O Ü
N E Z R E M H C S F P O K F L D
E O T T Ü C R A M P S E R M H U
K S I S E B E C S E M F H O S R
C E F T U M E E B T G P G Z C C
O T R E C H T L D L I M U H H H
P E E D V E E N K L Q Ä O I L F
D B P I B E F H G E N R C A A A
N A P A D E R N C O I K Ä U G L
I I I R L I P K I A E T S J A L
W D R R O G S T Ä N D S H E N S
P I G H C R K T P L C A S S F I
J F I E B E R O R H T U E H A W
N I H A F L X H L O A U V H L R
I A T N E L Y A C N K R N T L A
H E I Ä L A G A A L L E R G Y D
```

ALLERGY	ALLERGIE
CHICKENPOX	WINDPOCKEN
COLD	ERKÄLTUNG
COUGH	HUSTEN
CRAMPS	KRÄMPFE
DIABETES	DIABETES
DIARRHEA	DURCHFALL
FEVER	FIEBER
FLU	GRIPPE
HEADACHE	KOPFSCHMERZEN
INFECTION	INFEKTION
NAUSEA	ÜBELKEIT
NOSEBLEED	NASENBLUTEN
RASH	AUSSCHLAG
STROKE	SCHLAGANFALL

Study these maladies so you can develop a healthy bilingual vocabulary.

```
E R T N K I N I J D K M S Ä A Z
T N E D I C C A V H V A E S F N
Y I E E N I A R G I M E T B V E
Y N T A E T E T R H R H R I E Z
S T M E T U M U T U M U R O R R
P S N I H N S S T A C N S V S E
E P I R G C A C H H T N E A T M
L M A T K R A F N I Z R E H A H
I U R Z G R Ä H D C B E A M U C
P M P I F E Z N C R S S O E C S
E I S P E L I P E A P A A A H N
T P R E L L U N G T M M G S U E
R U S A N I N R U B U O U L N G
A R F B R U I S E C M C T E G A
I N E D N U W T T I N H C S P M
U S S G E M I N E T R R E L A O
```

ACCIDENT	UNFALL
ASTHMA	ASTHMA
BRUISE	PRELLUNG
BURN	VERBRENNUNG
CUT	SCHNITTWUNDE
EPILEPSY	EPILEPSIE
FRACTURE	BRUCH
HEART ATTACK	HERZINFARKT
MEASLES	MASERN
MIGRAINE	MIGRÄNE
MUMPS	MUMPS
SPRAIN	VERSTAUCHUNG
STOMACH ACHE	MAGENSCHMERZEN
VIRUS	VIRUS

Here are some basic questions and terms that you might hear frequently used in any language. Why? Because. Find these questionable terms and phrases below.

```
S N H A C R S D H E D C O Y S O
T I E W E I W E O A T T K H P N
M S I F O L H O W M U C H O O T
T E I H L I L I W O E S H W H W
O E V R M E E O Y O E H H M O T
V S M C I V H E H T K A O A Ä N
N U E P I D R R S J T M W N N M
E A W E L A S I I T L O F Y Z H
U C L A W E T E I M U R A W F H
M E O O N Ä H M T Ä U S R Ä I O
H B H D P N E U E H M D T O A A
R W T S E I N S O A E W T V E I
O R E H S A W D R Y I G V O R T
H I W I E V I E L E N T E E E S
W O T K L H W Y H W H A T I H T
N P I N T I N O D O E A C F W A
```

BECAUSE	WEIL
HOW	WIE
HOW ARE YOU	WIE GEHT ES DIR
HOW FAR	WIE WEIT
HOW MANY	WIE VIELE
HOW MUCH	WIE VIEL
CAN YOU HELP ME	kannst DU MIR HELFEN
WHAT	WAS
WHAT TIME IS IT	WIE SPÄT IST ES
WHEN	WANN
WHERE	WO
WHO	WER
WHY	WARUM

Table for two? Welcome to our Learn with Word Search restaurant. On the menu are the following helpful and delicious restaurant related words. Enjoy!

```
Q I C R S N Ä C Ä D E M I C G H
E I W E E S I E P S R O V E P Ü
T T E T N M N T S Ü T I K F G O
H H T I S O O E S N F C N N N R
E C R A N O N V T A Ü L U K U F
B I A W I R P I T T F N U T N R
I R K P K T A E S S E K O N H F
L E N T P S R H K I I I A H C C
L G I R A E Ü I D N L L V E E H
A T E E N R T E N E Ä S E R R O
E P W S F O B I T K S R D N E B
O U I S M H Ü T Z R G S T I I S
U A B E N D E S S E N E E E D W
N H N D I N N E R T R H L R G T
E Ü E S R U O C N I A M L D T Ä
M I T T A G E S S E N A C T I G
```

APPETIZER	VORSPEISE
BREAKFAST	FRÜHSTÜCK
DESSERT	DESSERT
DINNER	ABENDESSEN
DRINK	GETRÄNK
EAT	ESSEN
LUNCH	MITTAGESSEN
MAIN COURSE	HAUPTGERICHT
MENU	MENÜ
NAPKINS	SERVIETTEN
RESTROOMS	TOILETTEN
THE BILL	DIE RECHNUNG
TIP	TRINKGELD
WAITER	BEDIENUNG
WINE LIST	WEINKARTE

After that delicious meal it is time to head
back to the hotel and relax. Here is a list
of hotel words that might help give you a good
night's sleep.

```
Ü R E H E S N R E F A B N S L T
Ä U T O G C Z A Ö D T T O M F O
R A I Ü A H I T Ä T E M O G G I
H C U E G L M V E T O H O T E L
N T S B G D M L R O Y S R W C E
L O H R U T E N R E T N I G I T
H E I U L V R B R E S N Y D V T
C L S T I O I E K L S M N H R E
U E R S P L Z N D C N U O I E N
T W I I Ü E A E T T Ä T I O S P
D O N D P L C M T E E P Y T R A
N T R T B K H E M L R I E E E P
A Y I O E U B C R R A N K G M I
H O Ö N I C H T S T Ö R E N M E
N T T O I L E T P A P E R T I R
G O I D U T S S S E N T I F Z W
```

BED	BETT
BLANKETS	DECKEN
DO NOT DISTURB	bitte NICHT STÖREN
GYM	FITNESSSTUDIO
HOTEL	HOTEL
INTERNET	INTERNET
KEY	SCHLÜSSEL
LUGGAGE	GEPÄCK
RECEPTION	REZEPTION
ROOM	ZIMMER
ROOM SERVICE	ZIMMERSERVICE
SUITE	SUITE
TELEVISION	FERNSEHER
TOILET PAPER	TOILETTENPAPIER
TOWEL	HANDTUCH

Were you a good student? Here are some subjects that you may have studied long ago, or may be learning right now. Study these challenging subject translations.

```
S N Ä M T F Ä H C S E G H E T K
G E O G R A P H Y H N B I P U Q
N S I B I O L O G I E T H N G P
I E C H E M I E R S C I S Y H P
M W H S P G R E A T L T L Y E K
I R S C E O E R O O F R S Y C I
E U M C A N S S S R E I R G L S
C E E A I R I O C Y K T T O A U
N I D G T M P C L H S A H L N M
E N N Ä S H O S I I I S Y O G E
I E U N Y E Y N M D H C A I U D
C G K E M E D E O A E P H B A I
S N D T U R H O T C T M E T G Z
W I R T S C H A F T E H Ä B E I
O A E M I C L B U S I N E S S N
T F A H C S N E S S I W A E Ä A
```

ART	KUNST
BIOLOGY	BIOLOGIE
BUSINESS	GESCHÄFT
CHEMISTRY	CHEMIE
ECONOMICS	WIRTSCHAFT
ENGINEERING	INGENIEURWESEN
GEOGRAPHY	ERDKUNDE
HISTORY	GESCHICHTE
LANGUAGES	SPRACHEN
MATH	MATHE
MEDICINE	MEDIZIN
MUSIC	MUSIK
PHILOSOPHY	PHILOSOPHIE
PHYSICS	PHYSIK
SCIENCE	WISSENSCHAFT

Math. Some people love it, and some people hate it. Add these words to your vocabulary and multiply your language skills.

```
E N N O I T A C I L P I T L U M
P O O L E L L A R A P T G T B G
E I N I A T H C E R K N E S E L
R T K I T E M H T I R A O O E S
C A R G D K R A Q D D N M Y Q D
E K L N D O A A G D O E E Z U I
N I E U U I S R I I T F T U A V
T L L H C H V T T R L A R R T I
A P L C N I I I Y B S A I B I S
G I A I E O D V S T U T E I O I
E T R E N D O N N I H S C N N O
M L A L A L F E E M O J G S I N
U U P G U B Z U E P D N I O E L
L M E M N O I T C A R T B U S S
O B E J R S I E H C I E R E B B
V N E P C C E R U L E R P A A M
```

ADDITION	ADDITION
AREA	BEREICH
ARITHMETIC	ARITHMETIK
DIVISION	DIVISION
EQUATION	GLEICHUNG
GEOMETRY	GEOMETRIE
MULTIPLICATION	MULTIPLIKATION
PARALLEL	PARALLEL
PERCENTAGE	PROZENTSATZ
PERPENDICULAR	SENKRECHT
RULER	LINEAL
SUBTRACTION	SUBTRAKTION
VOLUME	VOLUMEN

It is estimated that globally there are over 100,000 flights per day. Here are some common airport related terms for you to learn while they try to find your lost baggage.

```
E S T C N H A B T R A T S H I S
T L I I N T E R N A T I O N A L
E A C T N E S G D I C H L I R A
X N K S B D F A Ü H U Ä L E L V
T O E E H S N A E L N E I H A I
D I T M O T L R H D F S U C N R
E T I O T F H A I G E B N S I R
P A R D Ä E F S N P U N A G M A
A N Y O I W C A A I I L O U R N
R R E T P H L S T T M S F L E K
T E G B I S S A I R C R A F T Ü
U T F E E R S F L U G Z E U G N
R N L X P H U A I R P O R T G F
E I L G R Ä B C P Y A W N U R T
S M O T S U C A E G A G G A B E
T T Z O M R R K F S P E A N G T
```

AIRCRAFT	FLUGZEUG
AIRPORT	FLUGHAFEN
ARRIVALS	ANKÜNFTE
BAGGAGE	GEPÄCK
CUSTOMS	ZOLL
DEPARTURES	ABFLÜGE
DOMESTIC	INLÄNDISCH
INTERNATIONAL	INTERNATIONAL
PASSPORT	REISEPASS
RUNWAY	STARTBAHN
SECURITY	SICHERHEIT
TAKEOFF	ABHEBEN
TERMINAL	TERMINAL
TICKET	FLUGSCHEIN

Farming has existed since 10,000 BC. If you work on a farm, or just like eating food, here are a some farm words for you harvest.

```
H Ä H N C H E N E K C I H C O I
X D P I H I Y P V X D R R D Z N
S T I E R A R E T S O O R A I B
C O G W I D H R Q I P T N C E C
H N L H U D I T O S R C O K G T
A E R C E W A L U A H A N O E Ä
F Z K S D S H U K R A R A S R Y
D N F N H A H T B U T T R L E H
I A A E O T O A S N W O C K F I
R L R A D R E F P T H B R Y A C
W F M C R A E D S B N U M T M A
L P E E H S N G L W T L E A V T
E Z R E E P Y O L Y N L A F L H
A T W L I U M I E T L H E M S N
D U N I W H B I I H H I N T M C
M N E E O E Y A O E T T Ä G A W
```

BULL	STIER
CHICKEN	HÄHNCHEN
COW	KUH
CROPS	NUTZPFLANZEN
DONKEY	ESEL
DUCK	ENTE
FARMER	LANDWIRT
GOAT	ZIEGE
HORSE	PFERD
LAMB	LAMM
PIG	SCHWEIN
ROOSTER	HAHN
SHEEP	SCHAF
TRACTOR	TRAKTOR
TURKEY	TRUTHAHN

Time to get out there and experience all there is to see. How do you prefer to explore a new city? Try exploring these highly rated sightseeing words.

```
O Ü O A R K M S O U V E N I R S
I N F O R M A T I O N A D E P T
L M S A E T O U R G U I D E N I
A B P N R S G C A M E R A V E E
H B A L H I K A V E O C E M I I
H Ü R S Ü R C A L C E M U T R N
H T K O F U O H M L U S S S E F
E C O U E O T A T E E I C T L O
V A O V S T C R S U R R R N A R
A M B E I I I U M U N A Y E G M
E C E N E G M I O Ü K G R M T A
O O D I R E C T I O N S E U S T
M R I R H U F P R U I N E N N I
W D U S E R I D A F L U X O U O
T E G E N E T N E M U N O M K N
I R E R H Ü F E S I E R S D D A
```

ART GALLERY	KUNSTGALERIE
CAMCORDER	CAMCORDER
CAMERA	KAMERA
DIRECTIONS	RICHTUNGEN
GUIDE BOOK	REISEFÜHRER
INFORMATION	INFORMATION
MAP	KARTE
MONUMENTS	MONUMENTE
MUSEUM	MUSEUM
PARK	PARK
RUINS	RUINEN
SOUVENIRS	SOUVENIRS
TOUR GUIDE	REISEFÜHRER
TOURIST	TOURIST

Time to hit the beach for some sun, sand and surf. Below you will find a list of warm beach related words.

```
G E E A D G R L L V E Q L S T B
E L L I R B N E N N O S E V A W
P E T T B E V I N A A M F E H R
B R S E S O E A M N I C U G I S
R U A I H I L M D M O S A N D I
E C C S U N S B R N I S H S N S
H O D K T G U C E W A W C U U O
I H N E E R R O H W S S S N N N
H S A R G T F A S W E W G S H N
Y H S T O L I E S H I L A C A E
C B O Z E A N U R G A M L R G N
H A T C N Y G X A S O A M E R C
I I G D N A R T S S U R F E N R
H K H W E N A E C O G A M N N E
U I P S F T S E N G C I A O U M
A P I T L C H E I D E I Z A N E
```

BEACH	STRAND
BUCKET	EIMER
HAT	HUT
OCEAN	OZEAN
SAND	SAND
SANDCASTLE	SANDBURG
SEA	MEER
SHOVEL	SCHAUFEL
SUN	SONNE
SUNGLASSES	SONNENBRILLE
SUNSCREEN	SONNENCREME
SURFING	SURFEN
SWIMMING	SCHWIMMEN
WAVES	WELLEN

Is the museum near or far? Is it expensive to get in or not? Start studying these opposite terms, and you may find out.

```
O S A C T T Q L A I S F O Z N T
L T I S Z S Y D L U Y B X B S F
I T K C L L N R F K I O E E S O
S A E N L L G E T F G T B N O S
L T I A Y M I E Z U W E S O R C
A S E E F P M H T R E G H I G H
A S L E A O D L C R U N O I I L
B V L E U H O H L O O K B O R E
E R O R E W H D R A H C L F D C
A I S G G M R H A R T L K E E H
F A E T S Y F T I E R B L E I T
T I M S J E L X W W O R R A N N
T U D S Y N W E I C H A A Y M A
T T S M E B A D N O S O E S D S
O I I H T M E A C G S E R Y O S
K L T S N A O H D T O F K O L E
```

BIG	GROSS
SMALL	KLEIN
WIDE	BREIT
NARROW	ENG
TALL	HOCH
SHORT	KURZ
HIGH	HOCH
LOW	NIEDRIG
GOOD	GUT
BAD	SCHLECHT
WET	NASS
DRY	TROCKEN
HARD	HART
SOFT	WEICH

Would you be opposed or in favor of some more
opposite words? For better or worse, here
are some more words to study and find.

```
T O P H P T G G R S A U B E R W
X B I L L I G I T H C I R C R N
J S S I E H G P K L N H C O I E
F S H B Z H C G O C A H N T N S
T D I R T Y N S E W E G N E N S
A D C E E U E K L A L R P I L O
S L E U E D A E P A C O D U A L
O V T E I L L L O I F E T Q N H
F S M T T U U O O S P C O O G C
D D R T B R S H E F I N I F S S
D G Z N W D T D R T G S A F A E
D B H J I T E E D I Y S P E M G
T I O M R E W W L E T R H N E I
P H E E H G O T O H F L M F O H
V E N E N M T Z C L S P E A I U
A I B M S E X P E N S I V E L R
```

FAST	SCHNELL
SLOW	LANGSAM
RIGHT	RICHTIG
WRONG	FALSCH
CLEAN	SAUBER
DIRTY	DRECKIG
QUIET	RUHIG
NOISY	LAUT
EXPENSIVE	TEUER
CHEAP	BILLIG
HOT	HEISS
COLD	KALT
OPEN	OFFEN
CLOSED	GESCHLOSSEN

They say that opposites attract. See if you are attracted to the list of opposite words below. Find them in the grid, or don't.

```
H V N O T R K T W K R A D L O L
I G D U U Ü Q R W E N G L E T O
L N O N E A C A W S A A A T P A
E I N F A C H H G N D K I H P V
K N I T A S C N Q S E H R X S E
N N H Y Y S A H C H A E E N R P
U I T S A F W S L E E D E H X E
D G A A N T H G I L E D E C P Y
I E I A F H C A O L C K N T K A
C B M W E O S T A R K N E E H Ü
K Ü O P B I A T M E T O O N U G
E T Ü Ü T N L S K Z E F D Ü N N
A I E G C Y D E A A I E U N V O
A B Y T G E H M R O G C R L O R
Y T S U T E T D I F F I C U L T
F E Q R N S R Q N S O O E T L S
```

FULL	VOLL
EMPTY	LEER
NEW	NEU
OLD	ALT
LIGHT	HELL
DARK	DUNKEL
EASY	EINFACH
DIFFICULT	SCHWER
STRONG	STARK
WEAK	SCHWACH
FAT	DICK
THIN	DÜNN
BEGINNING	ANFANG
END	ENDE

An antonym is a word opposite in meaning to another. A synonym is a word that has the same or similar meaning to another word. Find the antonyms from the word list in the puzzle grid.

```
E V O N O T U O H T I W R S L H
H F I O Ü Ä G N I O H N E Ä Ü H
O C A D H P H M Ü N Ü Ü S E T L
Y H O W S S A D H N R J R I S A
E T E N T S W E H A G E W F D T
R Ä D H K E Ä E E Ü H Ü H A S E
E R E H R A F N U T S A L R I H
H L Z E U I Ü D I C S F E B O O
H D T S L O N O O P E U I I U V
C F S R N F E S D R Z E R R T N
A E T E N E L R N E T I R E S H
N I E O E E E A S I I Y N R I T
N A O E C T O E C H H O L N D P
S E H N L Ä Ä E O B E F O R E U
N E W O N L D Z U L E T Z T A N
C A S I L T Y S U X E I L R O E
```

NEAR	NAH
FAR	FERN
HERE	HIER
THERE	DORT
WITH	MIT
WITHOUT	OHNE
BEFORE	VORHER
AFTER	NACHHER
EARLY	FRÜH
LATE	SPÄT
INSIDE	INNEN
OUTSIDE	AUSSEN
FIRST	ZUERST
LAST	ZULETZT

MATERIALS

We encounter many different materials on a daily basis. Some are strong enough to hold up buildings and others are soft and flexible. Here is a list of common materials to choose from as we continue to build your language skills.

```
C O N C D N S H L R L E E T S B
O G S L I X T F A A U S W I E V
N S O S A S O H I A L H A T S M
C G P A A T N R R E P P O C T G
R S E N P L E L E E D N O T W D
E I D D L T G M T Y F L E O D E
T L U A A D G T A Q T P O W B F
E B T M S D N O M A I D U G A F
H E J S T F H I U H T H A K L O
M R I E I N O Y N L E F Z T U T
U E B O C N A N I T A L P U A S
E N I N H L I M T T O E E I N T
N V N K C E L G A H R E V L I S
J I I E T L W S L I I A D I N
M V V S T N T E P A D W P L N U
U T X L T O R L E T S I S O L K
```

CLAY	LEHM
CONCRETE	BETON
COPPER	KUPFER
DIAMOND	DIAMANT
GLASS	GLAS
GOLD	GOLD
MATERIAL	MATERIAL
METAL	METALL
PLASTIC	KUNSTSTOFF
PLATINUM	PLATIN
SAND	SAND
SILVER	SILBER
STEEL	STAHL
STONE	STEIN
WOOD	HOLZ

See if you can handle another shipment of common materials. Be sure to handle each one with care.

```
V L H R N F N D N N R E O E N W
D A E D E L S T A H L E D E R O
G H N A N E D O B B S T I U S T
N D L A D G B P R R N O P P T U
R W R L T E E A L A R O M R A M
D G U M M I M W T S U D T B I P
A H L U T Z T H A S B A T R N B
B T A G O R N P Y C B M N I L A
L M H R N T Y G A U E S E C E U
E R L Y H I I E R P R M M K S M
I E H I I R S T D E E S E T S W
S B S S O E C S A O H R Z N S O
E E S N E S Y T E N A T H E T L
N O T T O C E R A M I C A A E L
H V A L U M I N I U M U P E E E
R C E N H E Z K M U N I M U L A
```

ALUMINUM	ALUMINIUM
BRASS	MESSING
BRICK	ZIEGEL
CEMENT	ZEMENT
CERAMIC	KERAMIK
COTTON	BAUMWOLLE
IRON	EISEN
LEAD	BLEI
LEATHER	LEDER
MARBLE	MARMOR
PAPER	PAPIER
RUBBER	GUMMI
SOIL	BODEN
STAINLESS STEEL	EDELSTAHL
TITANIUM	TITAN

We've made it through the first half of the book. Time to stop and have something to drink. Can we suggest one of the following?

```
D R U M V W H I T E W I N E D O
C A P P U C C I N O M S N N T N
A K D O W R H G V Y T O I I A I
N D L E B R A N D Y D E G W G C
M O T I T P M E O T W N H D R C
L V N E M I P K E T A I A E N U
F Q E A L S A I O E S T E R I P
F A H C T F G R D K P B E E B P
U C H E F Y N I E W S S I E W A
D H A E A H E Y G T N E I F A C
Z A E H S M R K D H A E A F S E
A D B R O H S H S E C W G O S X
E S C E E W H I R I L C E C E H
L H D K S T T M U W H B I E R Y
S G L S F F S J K D E W E V E A
O A T A C A T G G A E H O W N F
```

BEER	BIER
BRANDY	BRANDY
CAPPUCCINO	CAPPUCCINO
CHAMPAGNE	CHAMPAGNER
COFFEE	KAFFEE
GIN	GIN
JUICE	SAFT
MILK	MILCH
RED WINE	ROTWEIN
RUM	RUM
TEA	TEE
VODKA	WODKA
WATER	WASSER
WHISKEY	WHISKEY
WHITE WINE	WEISSWEIN

Review Jumble: The translations in the word list below have been scrambled. Draw lines between the left and right columns to find the correct translations.

```
A D R E I Z E H N E E T R U O F
E I E R D E N H V F E I G H T E
T N E V E L E T V I E R Z E H N
Y A R T F Z B S Ü F J Ö S Ö I I
Q O H E F E E L F T L H C L R N
V C T N I V I H W E C Ö V O T G
A W Ü O E I S E N E F Ü W I E N
L F R N W F L O S N A T D Z E F
N O O R Z V Q E Ü I U F T U N R
D I H U E D R F C L X R N Ö P A
K W T E R G A E W Ü N I S L T R
E A Ö L N P I T E W Ü Ü E D E W
Ü F H S A Ö Ö S D A S P R P R H
E R R E H I E A I D S I R D Y G
S O T T W Ö T O E C O X G Ö V V
G L M I I S D A I G G Ü A T E T
```

ONE	DREI
TWO	NEUN
THREE	EIN
FOUR	FÜNFZEHN
FIVE	VIERZEHN
SIX	ZWÖLF
SEVEN	ACHT
EIGHT	ELF
NINE	ZWEI
TEN	FÜNF
ELEVEN	SIEBEN
TWELVE	ZEHN
THIRTEEN	DREIZEHN
FOURTEEN	VIER
FIFTEEN	SECHS

Review Time: Draw lines between the English word on the left and the corresponding translation on the right. Refer back to the original puzzle if you need help.

```
T R E D N U H N E E T N E V E S
N W Y T R I H T O B I C M D E E
J T E M Y E T G G I N W I G A C
D C E N J T I H M Ü L Ü L T H H
N Y N D T Z H ß U F T L L V O Z
A T T I F Y W G I N H Ü I E O I
S R Y N A Y N I I G D X O M N G
U O Ü T L H T Z E E I R N H I Y
O F A N X ß V N E U N Z E H N T
H I C N H I E A E H D Z N D E E
T F H E E E S W E V T T T U T N
I T T R T Ü Z Z Y H E S U I E I
T Y Z X S W B H C P H S G I E N
H I I E B E ß A C T A U S E N D
G S G E I G H T E E N Q M G A T
U N E S G I Z B E I S F M U A G
```

SIXTEEN	TAUSEND
SEVENTEEN	SECHZEHN
EIGHTEEN	SIEBZEHN
NINETEEN	NEUNZEHN
TWENTY	ACHTZEHN
THIRTY	NEUNZIG
FORTY	DREIßIG
FIFTY	ACHTZIG
SIXTY	FÜNFZIG
SEVENTY	VIERZIG
EIGHTY	HUNDERT
NINETY	MILLION
HUNDRED	SECHZIG
THOUSAND	SIEBZIG
MILLION	ZWANZIG

Review Jumble: The translations in the word list below have been scrambled. Draw lines between the left and right columns to find the correct translations.

```
U G E M T H Z S E L O C T P H L
I A A A E E E G O Q S C I H M I
G T N T D I A B A I I S G T O F
A R H Y S T E F R I D A Y D N G
T E M H I M H C O W T T I M D X
S I O E A T A G T N W U N I A D
R E R U N T U S O O E R E E Y N
E F G T R S H M D N D D L X E W
N L E E E M O U W I N A U S S D
N A N H T W T N R E E Y Y U T W
O N C E S U E E N S S N N V E T
D O D N E K E E W T D D S E R H
W I E S G O H O E S A A K T D U
O T D A Y C S L A Y Y G Y W A G
N A T I O N A L H O L I D A Y G
Y N Y W O R R O M O T T S L W I
```

MONDAY	GESTERN
TUESDAY	DONNERSTAG
WEDNESDAY	MITTWOCH
THURSDAY	FREITAG
FRIDAY	SONNTAG
SATURDAY	WOCHE
SUNDAY	SAMSTAG
WEEKEND	NATIONALFEIERTAG
NATIONAL HOLIDAY	MONTAG
TODAY	DIENSTAG
TOMORROW	WOCHENENDE
YESTERDAY	HEUTE
WEEK	TAG
DAY	MORGEN

Review Time: Draw lines between the English word on the left and the corresponding translation on the right. Refer back to the original puzzle if you need help.

```
Ä E Y W T S E P T E M B E R L E
A N T T O R O H C R A M O N T H
R R Ä A K C O C A N J A N U A R
A E A N T I G U E W T O P Z A H
E B B O O S R O C S V P Z R S L
Y M B M B B U M U E S A P R I L
D E E L E A N G M I N V E I Ä L
R T I F R C U B U N Q B G N H M
F P Z J L A E T R A M A R D A T
T E H A I R A D N E L A C Y D V
O S B H E A E E Z T D E A S G O
W A W R E B M E V O N N I D S N
S L Y L U J D O I P Ä U E I H I
S E Q T J A N U A R Y J H L N O
F N T L W X R H M B G E G U A H
H I T O A U G Y R T O N J J L K
```

JANUARY	APRIL
FEBRUARY	AUGUST
MARCH	SEPTEMBER
APRIL	OKTOBER
MAY	FEBRUAR
JUNE	JANUAR
JULY	MÄRZ
AUGUST	JAHR
SEPTEMBER	JULI
OCTOBER	DEZEMBER
NOVEMBER	JUNI
DECEMBER	MAI
CALENDAR	NOVEMBER
MONTH	MONAT
YEAR	KALENDER

Review Jumble: The translations in the word list below have been scrambled. Draw lines between the left and right columns to find the correct translations.

```
U A O I I N Y N C I I D U A N J
O A T H C A N A C H M I T T A G
N T L P I M Z M F M S D E H U A
O R S Ü H E R B S T O C R T T T
O E E N F W D O A E M R Y S H H
N D C M Ü S G N E A M O G O G S
R N O T M F M E U U E L N E I D
E U N Q R U O H W T R D E A N R
T H D E C G S I Ü U S T A V T T
F R Ü H L I N G O M U G C C W E
A H A L L T D I O N I T E W E U
L A C E E S P R I N G N E I O D
A J I R Y H N M O N T H U N E E
T D O A E I S E K U N D E T R Y
Ü S D T N H E Z R H A J S E E S
T I H G F T X Y T Ü Z G W R A R
```

WINTER	STUNDE
SPRING	WINTER
SUMMER	JAHRZEHNT
AUTUMN	JAHRHUNDERT
SECOND	FRÜHLING
MINUTE	MINUTE
HOUR	HERBST
DAY	NACHT
MONTH	JAHR
YEAR	SEKUNDE
MORNING	MONAT
AFTERNOON	NACHMITTAG
NIGHT	TAG
DECADE	SOMMER
CENTURY	MORGEN

Review Time: Draw lines between the English word on the left and the corresponding translation on the right. Refer back to the original puzzle if you need help.

```
T J E ß ß M ß B H A T F F A P Ü
O I M U D M E H E U N ß Ü L S E
F S O T L A H M ß N N E S N O T
M A O E B O L E S H T N E Ü M B
A H N R L Ü E L D R T R R R A T
G S A R T T T N R E F Z E G G I
E U O V Ü Y E E A Ü ß P G O E T
N T O R O T D E G ß I E W L N W
T A I F W Q L D A N L Y P D T K
A I Y H K Z Ü D K B A R H N A E
T S E C W Y V Z N O U R D G ß G
P I A E U A L B L P E T O L S X
B L U E I N W O R B Y L Y I O F
B V O B O C D Ü L Ü D L E L E C
Y E L L O W D I L E N G R A U S
Z R A W H C S A O R A N G E E ß
```

BLACK	SCHWARZ
BLUE	GRAU
BROWN	BRAUN
CYAN	SILBER
GOLD	ORANGE
GREY	GRÜN
GREEN	ROT
MAGENTA	GOLD
ORANGE	LILA
PINK	ZYAN
PURPLE	MAGENTA
RED	ROSA
SILVER	WEIß
WHITE	BLAU
YELLOW	GELB

Review Jumble: The translations in the word list below have been scrambled. Draw lines between the left and right columns to find the correct translations.

```
H T O R E C T A N G L E G E K O
N K R E I S A L O F A L C A D D
E B U C P H R L G C Ü G F I E H
E E T H I E D L A P T N M G E P
K C E T H C A D T D C A F A A D
I R N E H V U S N Y R I G E L S
E Q O C O D Q O E Y A R T O C R
R O C K G I M D P C S T F S N K
A O T E R A I S E T H T Ü D E R
U O B R I M T T R H V S E H D E
Q T C D A A Z Y L I N D E R N D
S I F R R N A E N S Z X E C N N
G T Y Ü A T F M S O A I S Y K I
N P R N A R A K U G E L A V O L
E Q Ü R Ü M E Q O C E L H H Y Y
B Y L W L S L N K H E L C R I C
```

CIRCLE	RECHTECK
CONE	SECHSECK
CUBE	KUGEL
CYLINDER	ZYLINDER
DIAMOND	KEGEL
HEXAGON	DIAMANT
OCTAGON	PYRAMIDE
OVAL	OVAL
PENTAGON	WÜRFEL
PYRAMID	KREIS
RECTANGLE	ACHTECK
SPHERE	DREIECK
SQUARE	STERN
STAR	QUADRAT
TRIANGLE	FÜNFECK

Review Time: Draw lines between the English word on the left and the corresponding translation on the right. Refer back to the original puzzle if you need help.

```
U T O H R F O A D O C G C O F O
N G D A T E U H V A T I H Y B Q
O N R A E G M W I N O I G I V A
S E L R E G D O N P H A U Z E D
E F R Z Ä H N E N R E F E A K O
H G I T A V G G K T A T P E F U
S C S M U N D N N B E B T V H A
A N S T A H E U A C D T R U O Ä
L T E W I G V Z S Y Ä Ä S I A O
E D H F O R E H E A D W I P M L
Y T P F T R N S C H I N X O I H
E O W H T N B E I M M T U P T L
K N K N A E P E P C I T P E W C
O G L I Ä I C E Y C H E E K R I
A U G E N B R A U E N T M N X M
E E Y E L N H N F O Ä T S O G D
```

CHEEK	KOPF
CHIN	GESICHT
EAR	OHR
EYE	AUGENBRAUEN
EYEBROWS	HAAR
EYELASHES	WIMPERN
FACE	KINN
FOREHEAD	LIPPEN
HAIR	WANGE
HEAD	NASE
LIPS	MUND
MOUTH	STIRN
NOSE	ZUNGE
TEETH	ZÄHNE
TONGUE	AUGE

Review Jumble: The translations in the word list below have been scrambled. Draw lines between the left and right columns to find the correct translations.

```
M L T Ü F I Y A L P V C T S E O
H E Z R A W T S U R B H L I R E
S E N I E B I R E R T U N D L H
H D H D E T E D E Y D B N G F E
O K S Y E L L B O G E N E E E H
U N W I A U P U M E N L A R M I
L E R A O W P C H U E I L H Z U
D L I H T O I E O C H T F I W X
E E S A U B N ß F A S T C U A M
R G T L X L G I N I V E E A ß T
B D A U M E N D A H E H T M Ü V
L N V P T G E W E O V P A D H E
A A I F E O T E M A O E P O N E
D H Ü R T F O E I E N D M H H L
E H E E Y N E F G H I T R T Ü N
Z J S C H U L T E R B L A T T M
```

ARM	HANDGELENK
ELBOW	ZEH
FINGER	DAUMEN
FOOT	TAILLE
HAND	BEIN
HIP	ARM
LEG	FUß
NIPPLE	HÜFTE
SHOULDER	ELLBOGEN
SHOULDER BLADE	SCHULTERBLATT
THUMB	HAND
TOE	SCHULTER
WAIST	BRUSTWARZE
WRIST	FINGER

Review Time: Draw lines between the English word on the left and the corresponding translation on the right. Refer back to the original puzzle if you need help.

```
N E W Ü E N E G Ü F L R S D H T
F N N I E N I E Ö O V W L L K Y
D A A L T T I P M R A O A E D T
F E B B D M H F R E H A H D A E
Ä L K L E Y R L H A Ö L Ü Ö E C
E E C N D L I A N R E G N I F E
T G A O Ö S Ü C R M E O E Ö Y R
E A B C S C R H R E P R Ö K E M
B N O Ä T Ü H S T S T S U R B E
C R S R C U E E K T A N A V E L
O E E K H I A L L C H E U N O H
G G E A N T A H K G O C K E Ü A
S N I K S Ü E Ö I N V T J N T S
P I T Z Z T I H E E A R T W W Ö
O F V O Ä Z T L D C H E A U E N
O B E R S C H E N K E L F P B A
```

ANKLE	FINGERNAGEL
ARMPIT	KÖRPER
BACK	HAUT
BODY	BRUST
BREAST	RÜCKEN
BUTTOCKS	KNÖCHEL
CALF	ACHSELHÖHLE
FINGERNAIL	UNTERARM
FOREARM	HALS
KNEE	WADE
NAVEL	KEHLE
NECK	GESÄSS
SKIN	OBERSCHENKEL
THIGH	NABEL
THROAT	KNIE

Review Jumble: The translations in the word list below have been scrambled. Draw lines between the left and right columns to find the correct translations.

```
B L O O D Ü B C O W J N V S M T
M A R O N O O N E S K E E A Ü E
A R F M T U L R E V I L G T T N
N G F U S A A M Q N D E R N R I
E E Q S I O U R S G N A H N A T
A I E K O S L A R T E R I E N S
Ü N E E C E P D R H Y R E G R E
H T E L N P G N I T F B E R I T
H E E N E I S N I Q E E Z B H N
Ü S R N E O C Ü U A O R L A E I
N T D Z L V G D H L R U I F G L
D I L X P G M Ü C E T B M E E L
X N E E S U H D H C A M O T S A
P E H R T R H I D I C K D A R M
E S A E E E O E O E N L U N G S
E W E Ü R T P B O E A O B R O R
```

APPENDIX	GEHIRN
ARTERIES	ANHANG
BLOOD	LUNGE
BRAIN	MILZ
HEART	MUSKELN
KIDNEY	ARTERIEN
LARGE INTESTINE	VENEN
LIVER	DICKDARM
LUNGS	BLUT
MUSCLES	MAGEN
SMALL INTESTINE	LEBER
SPLEEN	HERZ
STOMACH	DÜNNDARM
VEINS	NIERE

Review Time: Draw lines between the English word on the left and the corresponding translation on the right. Refer back to the original puzzle if you need help.

```
H A K I R E M A D R O N S M T E
A T A C I R E M A H T R O N K P
T N O R D P O L R Ü Ä K U O I O
L R S D E E V A G O Q I T R T R
A O O A A D F Y N G U F H T N U
N T N E C R U A E M A I A H A E
T A N G I I G T T Ä T Z M P L L
I U N K I E T N I N O A E O T O
C Q A T U T E C E T R P R L A P
O E H R A N U N R G A S I E N H
C M O R I R I D B A N L C E N T
E P T T A T K Ü E H T Ä A Y T U
A I N I N L A T L Ä N N L T T O
N O S O D S A K I R E M A D Ü S
K A C I R F A W T S Ü D P O L Ä
A M P A C I F I C O C E A N H Y
```

AFRICA	BREITENGRAD
ANTARCTICA	SÜDPOL
ASIA	PAZIFIK
ATLANTIC OCEAN	AFRIKA
CONTINENT	ANTARKTIS
EQUATOR	LÄNGENGRAD
EUROPE	ATLANTIK
LATITUDE	KONTINENT
LONGITUDE	EUROPA
NORTH AMERICA	SÜDAMERIKA
NORTH POLE	NORDAMERIKA
PACIFIC OCEAN	ÄQUATOR
SOUTH AMERICA	ASIEN
SOUTH POLE	NORDPOL

Review Jumble: The translations in the word list below have been scrambled. Draw lines between the left and right columns to find the correct translations.

```
S  T  F  E  E  R  L  A  R  O  C  ß  Ü  A  T  H
R  R  T  G  J  E  C  R  E  E  Z  L  T  S  C  N
W  I  Q  L  L  O  T  O  I  S  M  E  E  R  R  E
E  Ü  V  R  R  V  S  E  C  Z  K  I  A  E  E  S
A  T  S  E  R  O  F  A  A  A  C  O  D  N  H  T
C  L  B  T  R  L  L  H  L  X  A  R  N  C  C  T
R  V  Ü  A  E  C  J  E  G  V  T  D  A  T  S  O
Ü  O  E  R  R  A  F  T  S  U  Y  E  L  T  T  B
R  S  M  K  M  N  T  S  S  N  B  T  S  E  E  T
A  R  Ü  E  A  O  A  Ü  A  H  I  A  I  R  L  R
H  T  D  E  S  N  U  K  A  F  O  P  G  C  G  E
W  T  C  D  J  K  A  N  L  C  D  N  A  R  T  S
W  O  N  S  N  Ü  P  U  T  U  S  N  ß  E  B  E
T  E  Ü  N  E  O  ß  S  E  A  V  N  W  A  L  D
O  W  A  H  S  K  Ü  R  F  L  I  N  T  D  I  A
B  O  W  U  K  O  R  A  L  L  E  N  R  I  F  F
```

BEACH	WÜSTE
CITY	MEER
COAST	VULKAN
CORAL REEF	SEE
CRATER	KÜSTE
DESERT	GLETSCHER
FOREST	WALD
GLACIER	INSEL
ISLAND	FLUß
LAKE	STRAND
MOUNTAIN	OZEAN
OCEAN	KRATER
RIVER	KORALLENRIFF
SEA	STADT
VOLCANO	BERG

Review Time: Draw lines between the English word on the left and the corresponding translation on the right. Refer back to the original puzzle if you need help.

```
U A H D N H S N U S N R O R A Ö
I E T E O Q T H N D A S S Ö A Ö
T T G U Y G O D F M I Ö T I V H
R E N N O D I E R E E M R A W L
R F F I L Z U D S E T E U R L A
R I O O T C H O N M E E N H C S
T T C I H U C E L I K L E A I C
Ö S L T P U O M S C W V B L R L
G B N A K I R R U H O T E I T I
T E Y O K A E R T E B O L G E O
R W S D W D D G I N N O S H M B
G Ö A A N T N T S C I M S T O P
R L G U F I H E U T A D S N R R
T K H U A O W Z N R R N I I A L
A T L R R E G E N B O G E N B E
L A W S U G Ö U Y I T E H G C P
```

BAROMETRIC pressure	NEBEL
CLOUDY	REGEN
COLD	KALT
FOG	SONNIG
HOT	LUFTDRUCK
HUMID	DONNER
HURRICANE	REGENBOGEN
LIGHTNING	SCHNEE
RAIN	WARM
RAINBOW	HEISS
SNOW	FEUCHT
SUNNY	BEWÖLKT
THUNDER	BLITZ
WARM	HURRIKAN
WINDY	WINDIG

Review Jumble: The translations in the word list below have been scrambled. Draw lines between the left and right columns to find the correct translations.

```
W A R Z E N S C H W E I N T Ä Ö
F E L R H R D E L E F F A R I G
S C A L B E P R Z R H U G N E C
A C T J I O A N E Y H O R R S Ö
Ä R H B L R A A Ä F R M Z O U S
G H B I Y P O N Ä I P E L H M P
I I T E M E E G L D B L D S A A
R N C I Z P T L I R E E I A T V
A O H ß Ö Ä A S A A N P I N O I
F C E U I H W N G P W H D A P A
F E E A E A N E S O B A B O O N
E R T R R E P O L E T N A Ä P C
O O A T N A L I W L Ö T L N P R
E S H S R C O Ö W U L E E A I N
Ä O I D O N L A O S T R I C H A
G D T T N A F E L E O P A R D O
```

ANTELOPE	ANTILOPE
BABOON	GORILLA
CHEETAH	PAVIAN
CHIMPANZEE	GIRAFFE
ELEPHANT	NILPFERD
GIRAFFE	STRAUß
GORILLA	NASHORN
HIPPOPOTAMUS	LEOPARD
HYENA	WARZENSCHWEIN
LEOPARD	SCHIMPANSE
LION	ZEBRA
OSTRICH	HYÄNE
RHINOCEROS	GEPARD
WARTHOG	LÖWE
ZEBRA	ELEFANT

Review Time: Draw lines between the English word on the left and the corresponding translation on the right. Refer back to the original puzzle if you need help.

```
C W F M S H P O W R E E F L O W
N O T G C U G N H T E U H A N O
X L R L E N A S I F C R Q R F Z
S F E E E H M T H D A H E W S
D L G N L M O O S E W K T L H L
R E I T L U A M R T Z N C A E T
P D T A S J M C K L W T T M T F
S E D E A P D Ä A N I I A F E S
I R N G G F N K Ä J G K T K S P
J M U G D G I A E E E I C A A Ä
I A H A U O U N R Ä B S I E B E
R U G R E I G G Ä B N Ä T R D N
Ä S U U S E N A A L Y Ä W Y D W
A M H C A T I R F K I R F H E F
V Q N N H R P O O Ä E I U E T N
R A E B R A L O P P E B D A M S
```

BAT	PINGUIN
CAMEL	FLEDERMAUS
CAT	ELCH
DOG	HUND
FOX	HASE
JAGUAR	MAULTIER
KANGAROO	KATZE
MOOSE	WOLF
MOUSE	FUCHS
MULE	KAMEL
PENGUIN	JAGUAR
POLAR BEAR	KÄNGURU
RABBIT	MAUS
TIGER	TIGER
WOLF	EISBÄR

Review Jumble: The translations in the word list below have been scrambled. Draw lines between the left and right columns to find the correct translations.

```
Q S E G C K X S N A K E R A T C
N C T A D N F N Q R A C C O O N
A E N I P U C R O P N X S B N Q
T U H L F K C K O A B T C I S W
U L T C M S O R T G I E E B C T
G E N Ö N D U U O N I W E E H B
N R T A I R G C K C H F S R L M
A R Ä L O N Ö T H C O C Q A A I
R I F B A Ö I H S I E D C M N T
O U R R Z E Ö L N T P K I A G A
B Q O E R R E V A E B M E L E O
R S S X N H A T A E K T U L E E
E G C C C S T W A R S C R N W G
H I H A M A L R H R P T A C K O
C E T T A R Ä B H C S A W B Ä N
N S F N R S C U E T S N O Ö V A
```

BEAVER	BIBER
BLACK BEAR	STACHELSCHWEIN
CHIPMUNK	BACKENHÖRNCHEN
CROCODILE	EULE
FROG	STINKTIER
LLAMA	RATTE
ORANGUTAN	FROSCH
OWL	WASCHBÄR
PORCUPINE	ORANG-UTAN
RACCOON	LAMA
RAT	SCHLANGE
SKUNK	KROKODIL
SNAKE	SCHWARZBÄR
SQUIRREL	EICHHÖRNCHEN

Review Time: Draw lines between the English word on the left and the corresponding translation on the right. Refer back to the original puzzle if you need help.

```
P H B W T I N T E N F I S C H W
I L I A U A E W F O F I S C H L
E A S U R L A W A I R O R A R M
H W D A T C H T N L A W L E E A
N T Ö ß L C E R D A R E M M U H
A R F L E O E L B E C O F O O O
E E Ö H E T ß O L S L R ß S T R
E W M I S E C B J A M P O I R A
Q H C E S T S S E C U P H D D K
N C E S O T I T L F I Q O I N I
K S N P M E A E L I R L U R N D
R O U R S Ö U R Y S P Q E L E G
A S E E H U N D F H S M A E Ö N
B I E C A R S E I I M E D L I Ö
B A Q S R W D N S U S E V E A I
E T Ö R K D L I H C S H L I F D
```

TURTLE	SEESTERN
CRAB	QUALLE
DOLPHIN	SCHILDKRÖTE
FISH	WALROß
JELLYFISH	HAI
LOBSTER	HUMMER
OCTOPUS	SCHWERTWAL
ORCA	HUMMER
SEA LION	TINTENFISCH
SEAL	SEELÖWE
SHARK	FISCH
SQUID	KRABBE
STARFISH	SEEHUND
WALRUS	WAL
WHALE	DELPHIN

Review Jumble: The translations in the word list below have been scrambled. Draw lines between the left and right columns to find the correct translations.

```
A A O O T E T D O A L C U O N A
D G R O ß V A T E R I R O A N G
R R E T S E W H C S I S T E R ß
E A E S S L Y ß F H N E O M W T
H N H T V C C T A I I N T H B W
T D I T T N E N M L K L I D N E
A M R E D U R B I E N J D E A H
F O H Y B O M M L R E R R R C P
D T R S T R A ß Y N E T E T E E
N H E P N F O O O ß Q T H T T N
A E D A U G H T E R H N T C L K
R R E R A E T J H C G E A U I E
G ß V E T H T E O E I F F N M N
N S O N L M O T H E R F D B S G
ß L A T O H ß L L C R E T A V O
T T O S D R A F A A R N ß S A H
```

AUNT	NEFFE
BROTHER	ELTERN
CHILDREN	GROßVATER
DAUGHTER	SOHN
FAMILY	VATER
FATHER	FAMILIE
GRANDFATHER	BRUDER
GRANDMOTHER	MUTTER
MOTHER	SCHWESTER
NEPHEW	NICHTE
NIECE	GROßMUTTER
PARENTS	TOCHTER
SISTER	ONKEL
SON	KINDER
UNCLE	TANTE

Review Time: Draw lines between the English word on the left and the corresponding translation on the right. Refer back to the original puzzle if you need help.

```
S C H W I E G E R M U T T E R W
S O N I N L A W H P T Z U E E A
C S L F H P D N N E G M T W T L
H I N N A M E H E E O H A L H N
W S G H R T D M A T G L E S C I
I T M R O O H N H U N N Z A O R
E E A S A S Y E A I A L U L T E
G R Ä S W N R D R B N R E J R T
E I E L E I D E Y I S K F M E H
R N L G N N H S G Z N U T G G G
V L Ä L A T K E O E E L H O E U
A A A R O W D E H N I D A E I A
T W G R J D H C L E T W D W W D
E I B E P Y D C G I R L H I H O
R F O T O Ä W Q S W N Y A C C G
W E Y E M N I R E G Ä W H C S A
```

BROTHER-IN-LAW	EHEMANN
BOY	SCHWAGER
DAUGHTER-IN-LAW	FRAU
FATHER-IN-LAW	SCHWÄGERIN
GIRL	ENKEL
GRANDDAUGHTER	SCHWIEGERSOHN
GRANDSON	SCHWIEGERTOCHTER
HUSBAND	SCHWIEGERVATER
MOTHER-IN-LAW	ENKELIN
SISTER-IN-LAW	JUNGE
SON-IN-LAW	SCHWIEGERMUTTER
WIFE	MÄDCHEN

Review Jumble: The translations in the word list below have been scrambled. Draw lines between the left and right columns to find the correct translations.

```
B W S E G N A H C O T T I D N I
G E B O N E K N E D O S E H E N
U C Z I A E C E E H C E M F F S
T H E A C R G W E T A T T F A E
P S D T H H T A O T R A M H L F
F E N E E L R B R E R A F L H X
R L E O D O E A L F Y A W V C V
E N R L Z S I N G E N I G C S T
D U Ö E S L P A I K S K R E Ö T
N R H N T O S I N G O E E C N E
H E A H T G T I T C R O N Y N K
B M G B L O H I H T R N C A E S
O D F L R T A E E A E E S O T U
W N H E O W N S I E K S A O T F
T E A T O F O L L O W S H L T Ö
I D U T O P A Y H T H E G P R M
```

TO ASK	WECHSELN
TO BE	FRAGEN
TO CARRY	ESSEN
TO CHANGE	LESEN
TO COOK	TRAGEN
TO EAT	FOLGEN
TO FOLLOW	SCHLAFEN
TO HEAR	SINGEN
TO PAY	WARTEN
TO READ	DENKEN
TO SEE	SEHEN
TO SING	HÖREN
TO SLEEP	KOCHEN
TO THINK	SEIN
TO WAIT	BEZAHLEN

Review Time: Draw lines between the English word on the left and the corresponding translation on the right. Refer back to the original puzzle if you need help.

```
H O A F W F R G F D H E L F E N
O A A N N E H C U S S A W T E K
I L S N E H C E R P S R E K R N
E S W E F D O E T M T A N O E O
D D T A U L N C K T K I W M E R
U N O R A R R I S A R O H E E E
R A E B K I G E F T T E M T F I
O T V E R S T E H E N O R M N S
F S O I E B T O D O T S T N E E
K R L T V R H O C O I H O C B N
O E O E R D C T H L O P C K A L
O D T N N A A A O E O E O F H I
L N N I I N V H T H L S M C B E
O U F U V E T E T O S P E A K B
T O D R I N K L L E S O T Y B E
T T S D I H S C H L I E S S E N
```

TO CLOSE	VERKAUFEN
TO COME	KOMMEN
TO DO	LIEBEN
TO DRINK	TUN
TO FIND	SCHLIESSEN
TO HAVE	FINDEN
TO HELP	TRINKEN
TO LOOK FOR	NEHMEN
TO LOVE	HELFEN
TO SELL	VERSTEHEN
TO SPEAK	ARBEITEN
TO TAKE	HABEN
TO TRAVEL	SPRECHEN
TO UNDERSTAND	ETWAS SUCHEN
TO WORK	REISEN

Review Jumble: The translations in the word list below have been scrambled. Draw lines between the left and right columns to find the correct translations.

```
T O W R I T E L T N E W O O T O
O N G Y M U V T E T O R U N G A
B Z E O D T O D A N C E E Y A Y
E N G B T L L W K E O L A B C E
A I R E E U S O N P L L D A S E
B E L A H G T O L O P A O R E N
L S V C E E U R W O K Ö R I R M
E E S L A L N I T T A N Z E N R
T G C P G T O B U Y U Ö N G E C
O A H G I T L T E A F N E P Ö E
W L R O S E O E V F E N T U Q A
A R E R S G L W N N N E S S I W
N E I L I U V E A O A N P D E Ö
T D B V K L N T N L A R T V I D
X N E S S A L R E V K E H S M X
I I N E H E G T T Y G L H E O I
```

TO BE ABLE TO	IN DER LAGE SEIN
TO BUY	GEBEN
TO DANCE	ÖFFNEN
TO GIVE	VERLASSEN
TO GO	KAUFEN
TO KNOW	WISSEN
TO LEARN	SPIELEN
TO LEAVE	GEHEN
TO OPEN	SCHREIBEN
TO OWE	WOLLEN
TO PLAY	LERNEN
TO RUN	GEHEN
TO WALK	RENNEN
TO WANT	SCHULDEN
TO WRITE	TANZEN

Review Time: Draw lines between the English word on the left and the corresponding translation on the right. Refer back to the original puzzle if you need help.

```
B Ü W R G O P Ä P I Ä D U R O E
R E T A W A M K Z D A E R B I S
O U O Z S Ü Ä I T U F L O U R E
T D T T R S O A L N C A E T N D
E Y A T E I E R A C O K N T V A
D Z D L R M F R Ü C H T E E E L
E H E O A H L F S T H S R R G O
V S S I M S C H O C O L A T E K
I I J U G L U S H T K A W T T O
W G T G G B N E I R L L G N A H
P V O I E A E U I E E D I R B C
B Ä Ä H H S R Ä N S L T E M L S
T T G L E F E R H Ü A F T H E I
M E R C N S I O A M L L E U S A
H T I A O U S G G E Z M A P B Ü
L R U R Ü E T S A G N G A T T Z
```

BREAD	ZUCKER
BUTTER	FRÜCHTE
CHEESE	FLEISCH
CHOCOLATE	KÄSE
EGGS	MEHL
FLOUR	BROT
FRUIT	BUTTER
MEAT	MILCH
MILK	GEMÜSE
PASTA	SCHOKOLADE
RICE	SALAT
SALAD	TEIGWAREN
SUGAR	REIS
VEGETABLES	EIER
WATER	WASSER

Review Jumble: The translations in the word list below have been scrambled. Draw lines between the left and right columns to find the correct translations.

```
H T P K S F E R F Ö A N R S E Y
H S R U J H H W Q D T N A O C U
C A A U O Z U T S Ö E I E O O N
S E T N G S L M M B G E B D T U
I A I P H O A T H A S D E E S C
E G R S U E Y L M Ö D G N T A M
L T P O R K B A N E E R L O L U
F R L C T G E I I P Ö N A A Z L
D S E I K O O C E E C H M Ä H T
N C N F O S C P W R N B M Ä E O
I B E E F I P Ä D E E Z H E P T
R T K N G E L Z I E H N P T U K
P X C I R C F I R I C P X L D Ö
E O I W T N A P E H U T Ö A O L
Z O H O N E Y K E S K E K S E E
A S C H W E I N E F L E I S C H
```

BEEF	RINDFLEISCH
BEER	HONIG
CAKE	KUCHEN
CHICKEN	KEKSE
COOKIES	SUPPE
HONEY	SCHWEINEFLEISCH
ICE CREAM	HÄHNCHEN
LAMB	BIER
OIL	ÖL
PEPPER	SALZ
PORK	WEIN
SALT	EIS
SOUP	PFEFFER
WINE	LAMM
YOGURT	JOGHURT

Review Time: Draw lines between the English word on the left and the corresponding translation on the right. Refer back to the original puzzle if you need help.

```
E N O L E M R E S S A W O S S V
G A O H P O M E G R A N A T E U
G E R L L U R T S T O G R P I N
P R U P E G N A R O N C W H R E
L M A I N M S E N O K E T C R R
A P N N H E R P L G I I S A E E
N O E E A M R E F N E A R E B E
T E E A P T M E T L N E H P W B
W N K P R L A R E A A R T P A L
G R A P E S A P N B W U F L R E
O I L L E U J A F U D I M M T D
E B L E B L U E B E R R I E S I
A U B E R G I N E S L S E L T E
E E N O R T I Z I D C I S O W H
N E R A P R I C O T I O B N O Y
T L D P U T H E I E N O M E L H
```

APRICOT	ANANAS
BLUEBERRIES	ORANGE
EGGPLANT	ERDBEEREN
GRAPES	PFLAUME
LEMON	WEINTRAUBEN
MELON	WASSERMELONE
ORANGE	ZITRONE
PEACH	APRIKOSE
PEAR	GRANATAPFEL
PINEAPPLE	BIRNE
PLUM	PFIRSICH
POMEGRANATE	MELONE
STRAWBERRIES	HEIDELBEEREN
WATERMELON	AUBERGINE

Review Jumble: The translations in the word list below have been scrambled. Draw lines between the left and right columns to find the correct translations.

```
A K I R P A P R E N Ü R G I F N
T A R E P P E P W O L L E Y E E
H K S A T O K R O E E U N K E H
G I N I H C C U Z E G H S E C C
E R O T E R P A P R I K A A H S
M P E R E D P E P P E R N H E R
I A U E Ü A S U N N F A E I R I
L P D O N N M O O A N I R N R K
Q R L A L P T L U A N R E I I Ü
B E G I K A E T B A E A E H E R
Y B T I M M T P A B I P B C S B
V L N O G E A N P X Y P M C A I
A E T I M P T S A E V L O U E S
S G N A F A A T E C R E R Z N F
W O E E T R T N E R E E B M I H
H B L A C K B E R R I E S O H W
```

APPLE	KÜRBIS
BANANA	ZUCCHINI
BLACKBERRIES	GELBER PAPRIKA
CANTALOUPE	ROTER PAPRIKA
CHERRIES	BROMBEEREN
FIG	KIRSCHEN
GREEN PEPPER	APFEL
LIME	TOMATE
PUMPKIN	HIMBEEREN
RASPBERRIES	GRÜNER PAPRIKA
RED PEPPER	FEIGE
TOMATO	HONIGMELONE
YELLOW PEPPER	BANANE
ZUCCHINI	LIMETTE

Review Time: Draw lines between the English word on the left and the corresponding translation on the right. Refer back to the original puzzle if you need help.

```
E  S  Q  E  O  F  Ü  E  I  B  E  E  T  S  R  H
E  S  A  I  L  O  C  C  O  R  B  F  A  E  E  Z
K  T  J  L  E  H  C  U  A  L  B  O  N  K  W  W
L  A  S  P  A  R  A  G  U  S  A  Ü  I  T  O  I
E  N  R  P  G  T  N  M  T  E  K  K  P  T  L  E
G  G  O  O  I  A  E  H  Ü  A  G  A  S  I  F  B
R  E  A  G  T  N  R  N  A  R  R  L  C  I  E
A  N  H  B  K  T  A  L  N  T  Ü  T  Y  E  L  L
P  S  T  O  B  H  E  C  I  I  N  O  R  N  U  M
S  E  H  E  F  A  E  S  H  C  K  F  Ü  U  A  I
O  L  E  T  T  U  C  E  A  H  O  F  B  C  C  W
B  L  N  T  Ü  H  C  R  H  O  H  E  E  S  V  O
S  E  Y  E  O  U  R  N  O  K  L  L  N  K  L  Ü
B  R  O  C  C  O  L  I  I  E  E  N  O  I  N  O
E  I  K  B  T  T  S  P  H  R  T  H  S  O  E  L
S  E  O  T  A  T  O  P  Y  J  L  A  A  Ü  T  K
```

ARTICHOKE	BLUMENKOHL
ASPARAGUS	ARTISCHOCKE
BEETS	SPARGEL
BROCCOLI	KOHL
CABBAGE	KAROTTE
CARROT	KARTOFFELN
CAULIFLOWER	STANGENSELLERIE
CELERY	ZWIEBEL
GARLIC	SPINAT
KALE	BROCCOLI
LETTUCE	SALAT
ONION	RÜBEN
POTATOES	GRÜNKOHL
SPINACH	KNOBLAUCH

Review Jumble: The translations in the word list below have been scrambled. Draw lines between the left and right columns to find the correct translations.

```
E U A C M O O R G N I N I D E T
I Y I S D F N E H C T I K O M W
P E W A R T E M N N W Ü R E O E
Z M C F I V G M Z Ü H K E H O G
W H P N V R E I A O A K N F R E
M Y A B E T T Z U A Ü Z E O G W
M O T B W F Ü S N C I N T A N S
G I O I A S E S H M S T R V I T
E A C R Y T N E M T R A P A V H
H I R O D N H E E F G U T W I R
N E S A R E R R O O F S H O L A
T B A B G M B F O I K N A D F F
D K E L L E R N W O H N U N G U
O M L D F S W E T E M N S I G Z
Ü S C H L A F Z I M M E R W E T
R N W J L B S H P C B H S A E N
```

APARTMENT	DACH
BASEMENT	RASEN
BATHROOM	SCHLAFZIMMER
BED	KELLER
BEDROOM	ZUFARHTSWEG
DINING ROOM	FENSTER
DRIVEWAY	WC
FENCE	HAUS
GARAGE	ZAUN
HOUSE	WOHNZIMMER
KITCHEN	BETT
LAWN	GARAGE
LIVING ROOM	KÜCHE
ROOF	ESSZIMMER
WINDOW	WOHNUNG

Review Time: Draw lines between the English word on the left and the corresponding translation on the right. Refer back to the original puzzle if you need help.

```
W T G T E W U V E D O M M O K T
W A S H I N G M A C H I N E R U
H W S Ä T D N S S C D I D E O L
C Ä N S F V R A O D U I G E N H
S S K I E I Y E W F L U T C L J
I C E H A R T W S E A A M A E V
T H M T A T H D B S D U M L U R
O E S D E Ä R A B O E A C P C A
I T A L L Y T U H E N R B E H G
L R I R E H A R C N Ä D T R T I
E O O R T T C H A N D E L I E R
T C S U S A T R E P P E O F R H
A K B R M D C A R P E T P A L I
B N I M A K T F I U A T Y M L D
L E I E N I H C S A M H C S A W
E R O V O R H A N G V G A L U L
```

BATHTUB
CARPET
CHANDELIER
CURTAIN
DRESSER
DRYER
FAUCET
FIREPLACE
LAMP
STAIRS
TABLE
TOILET
VACUUM
WASHING MACHINE

TREPPE
KRONLEUCHTER
TEPPICH
STAUBSAUGER
WÄSCHETROCKNER
WASCHMASCHINE
KOMMODE
BADEWANNE
KAMIN
WASSERHAHN
TOILETTE
TISCH
LAMPE
VORHANG

Review Jumble: The translations in the word
list below have been scrambled. Draw lines
between the left and right columns to find the
correct translations.

```
R D R E L Ü P S R R I H C S E G
O M N G S E S M W O O C R I E T
T I A I R E H S A W H S I D W Y
A R U T E C Y W O L L I P W E N
L R Y T T T E Z T A R T A M E R
I O V E N R S H C R I B H K K E
T R H R N O E N F I R I C N C F
N I S B F M H S R S A E A A R R
E A L E G E I P S O B R A F A I
V H N T S D D H Y H H H D G E G
N C K T U S O N C C N C E N F E
E I W S I W E S S A H S S I L R
K E C S E S A L O F F G K L S A
C H N R S W H A L L W A Y I T T
E P E I P Ü E E U C B H N E E O
D I K B K Q G R H T T K L C A R
```

CHAIR	SESSEL
CEILING FAN	OFEN
CHIMNEY	MATRATZE
CRIB	KISSEN
DESK	GESCHIRRSPÜLER
DISHWASHER	WASCHBECKEN
HALLWAY	GITTERBETT
MATTRESS	DECKENVENTILATOR
MIRROR	SCHREIBTISCH
OVEN	KÜHLSCHRANK
PILLOW	SPIEGEL
REFRIGERATOR	DUSCHE
SHOWER	SCHORNSTEIN
SINK	FLUR

Review Time: Draw lines between the English word on the left and the corresponding translation on the right. Refer back to the original puzzle if you need help.

```
A G L A S S S S I T N W E N W Ö
W T S E Ö M V P U A I R O F I A
F A E S S L Ö F F E L O F O N A
S B R E S S E M P E P P E R E T
O L V O L P Ü D O S F B T K G G
I E I N O Ö L H L E F F Ö L L L
E S E E G W F A C H A N E H A A
K P T O O Z M F T S R U T R S S
C O T B L P W U E E F I N K S F
E O E L W E I N G L A S O O W Ö
D N B H F V B T O S H Ö O O L V
H N E I Ö S E A C N I K P A N R
C D C H S L M E G H R Ö S C Ö Ü
S S H R L S M E R U E M A A T Ö
I T E E N E T T G C I R E D L U
T R R H T O L C E L B A T A Y Z
```

BOWL	TISCHDECKE
FORK	LÖFFEL
GLASS	TELLER
KNIFE	KRUG
MUG	PFEFFER
NAPKIN	WEINGLAS
PEPPER	SCHÜSSEL
PITCHER	SALZ
PLATE	TEELÖFFEL
SALT	SERVIETTE
SPOON	GLAS
TABLECLOTH	MESSER
TABLESPOON	GABEL
TEASPOON	ESSLÖFFEL
WINE GLASS	BECHER

Review Jumble: The translations in the word list below have been scrambled. Draw lines between the left and right columns to find the correct translations.

```
R E T T U M N E B U A R H C S R
U N T E R L E G S C H E I B E S
V R N S R E F S Ü I Q D L V Ä C
Ü Ü N E U U H C N E R W I W N H
X S C H L Ü S S E L E R A H W R
L C J L S G X A A G D S N A Ä A
A H I E H C D P E W Ä A S B Ä U
O R L G M N H R E M P S P L E B
D A H A M M E R E N E G E E S E
I U E N C D C S A R C P O I U N
E B A H D S S Z W U H I A S N Z
P E H A R B E A T E B O L T D I
I Ü L E A N A N U T R E B I A E
Ü T I N I G R G L Z V C Ü F I H
I L D L E I T E R E T N S T T E
P H O H G Z Ü N L T H A M M E R
```

BOLT	UNTERLEGSCHEIBE
DRILL	LEITER
HAMMER	ZANGEN
LADDER	BOHRER
LEVEL	SÄGE
NAIL	SCHRAUBENZIEHER
NUT	SCHRAUBE
PENCIL	SCHRAUBENMUTTER
PLIERS	BLEISTIFT
SAW	NAGEL
SCREW	SCHRAUBE
SCREWDRIVER	SCHLÜSSEL
TAPE MEASURE	WASSERWAAGE
WASHER	HAMMER
WRENCH	MESSBAND

Review Time: Draw lines between the English word on the left and the corresponding translation on the right. Refer back to the original puzzle if you need help.

```
T S S G L E T N A M E D A B H S
A G E B Y T B D Ü I U N C L C M
R S L O A S E O T D P T O H Ü C
S T R O H S S K R P A J A M A S
G D L A V S C E E H N L T E G C
O E I P F E V S R E T A E W S H
G N T E N O S S L D S A F U C L
Ü L D V L L W O K T L E B Z H A
L M R L E K E C C R G Ü E B U F
A O U T T S S K T K A Q F L H A
P P R N N O T S W T E W R H E N
D Ü I N A M E R Q Y D N A A H Z
G E A N M T E S O H L M C T E U
A A C H T T M T U H A A S H T G
L U Ü S C F H A N D S C H U H E
N Y F T N E G D A O M W S D L H
```

BATHROBE	KLEID
BELT	MANTEL
COAT	SCHAL
DRESS	SCHLAFANZUG
GLOVES	KRAWATTE
HAT	SHORTS
NECKTIE	BADEMANTEL
PAJAMAS	WESTE
PANTS	PULLOVER
SCARF	HUT
SHOES	SCHUHE
SHORTS	GÜRTEL
SOCKS	HOSE
SWEATER	SOCKEN
VEST	HANDSCHUHE

Review Jumble: The translations in the word list below have been scrambled. Draw lines between the left and right columns to find the correct translations.

```
O E T I U S C O E T E E U I E N
S K I R T H O S E N T R Ä G E R
G N U D I E L K H T D N E C N S
N U M N H H P B E E I I K C O R
G K Z V D E S K Z P L L F A R R
G I D N Z E S L O F A B W H N W
L N N C A L R N A C V A U E T R
C A I O A B S W E D H D T O I I
F B I H O S S R E D N E P S U S
S E R W T T U S S A A A A O S T
T N T A O O D S B U R N S R M W
I I A O C O L M N B D Z S H I A
E T B E G E R C E A D U X N W T
F W B E J A L E L H E G Q S S C
E H C S Ä W R E T N U J E N O H
L A R M B A N D T E K V O S H U
```

WRIST WATCH	ANZUG
BOOTS	ROCK
BOW TIE	STIEFEL
BRA	HEMD
BRACELET	JEANS
CLOTHING	SANDALEN
JEANS	HOSENTRÄGER
NECKLACE	UNTERWÄSCHE
SANDALS	BH
SHIRT	ARMBANDUHR
SKIRT	KLEIDUNG
SUIT	BADEANZUG
SUSPENDERS	FLIEGE
SWIM SUIT	HALSKETTE
UNDERWEAR	ARMBAND

Review Time: Draw lines between the English word on the left and the corresponding translation on the right. Refer back to the original puzzle if you need help.

```
C T M O U T H W A S H A M P O O
O O U R Q L A O H O H E R M K T
M O N M A U I A T A N E F O A U
B T D T M S M P I E N O N I E K
S H W U A P I R S O E T N G E H
T P A S O C D E I T A E L N A S
N A S O S R T T R K I I N U T U
A S S O Y O I L T A P C H L S R
R T E E A D L L E P P Ö K Ü A B
O E R H N P I F E N E P R P P H
D M N O B N M N L S S A A S N T
O U C Ö S Ü S L S A Z E O R H O
E F W E F T E A Ö O T T S A A O
D R N R I E T S R Ü B N H A Z T
S E A F Z A H N S E I D E H Ö E
A P T N A R O D O E D O G D D N
```

COMB	LIPPENSTIFT
CONDITIONER	SEIFE
CONTACT LENSES	KONTAKTLINSEN
DENTAL FLOSS	PARFÜM
DEODORANT	ZAHNPASTA
HAIR DRYER	ZAHNBÜRSTE
LIPSTICK	DEODORANT
MOUTHWASH	KAMM
PERFUME	FÖN
RAZOR	HAARSPÜLUNG
SHAMPOO	RASIERAPPARAT
SOAP	ZAHNSEIDE
TOOTHBRUSH	MUNDWASSER
TOOTHPASTE	SHAMPOO

Review Jumble: The translations in the word list below have been scrambled. Draw lines between the left and right columns to find the correct translations.

```
T T N S S F B F A R M U S E U M
S R N A T A E T O T A K I F V O
E P R E H E M U K H R H I A F W
K R G N M A K R E A N R T F L E
A E H T T T A R N R E R I E U K
U O C S R M R K A S W C E L G C
F L O I R A E A T M E A I U H Ü
H P E E F N I A P L R G C B A R
A S P U H F T N U E H E R H F B
U U T A C I O H S T D P P L E R
S W U A O H C T H T R E O U N I
W S M N D S T O S N A O U B S D
Ü W D T H I U T S O H T P A D G
L A T I P S O H U C P X I R O E
N M U S E U M N S R B Ü R O I H
V I U B S T A D I U M T A S N A
```

AIRPORT	SUPERMARKT
BAR	KAUFHAUS
BRIDGE	BAR
DEPARTMENT store	LEUCHTTURM
FARM	BAHNHOF
FIRE STATION	SCHULE
HOSPITAL	STADION
LIGHTHOUSE	KRANKENHAUS
MUSEUM	BRÜCKE
OFFICE	FLUGHAFEN
POST OFFICE	BAUERNHOF
SCHOOL	POSTAMT
STADIUM	BÜRO
SUPERMARKET	MUSEUM
TRAIN STATION	FEUERWACHE

Review Time: Draw lines between the English word on the left and the corresponding translation on the right. Refer back to the original puzzle if you need help.

```
P R H R E I V E R I E Z I L O P
O C B A B U R G E S C H Ä F T E
L O A I R O Y H T P P D C N O T
I F H M B B P R S H K R A P Y H
C F E O B L O E A N G R S R O E
E E Y S T R I R R U T T N T A
S E E R U E M O Y A B T L E Ä T
T S K T A A L E T O H I E R T E
A H R F C T H S I H H O L O I R
T O S Y I F E N S G E F U T S E
I P L P A R K M R V É K K S R T
O A P O T H E K E E P N C K E A
N Ä E S A O A H V C P A B N V E
L I Ä F O H D E I R F O E A I H
N U E P C E N M N É D O U B N T
U N F R E S T A U R A N T A U K
```

BANK	PARK
CASTLE	BANK
CEMETARY	BIBLIOTHEK
COFFEE SHOP	UNIVERSITÄT
HARBOR	GESCHÄFT
HOTEL	THEATER
LIBRARY	FRIEDHOF
OPERA HOUSE	BURG
PARK	CAFÉ
PHARMACY	OPERNHAUS
POLICE STATION	HAFEN
RESTAURANT	HOTEL
STORE	POLIZEIREVIER
THEATER	RESTAURANT
UNIVERSITY	APOTHEKE

Review Jumble: The translations in the word list below have been scrambled. Draw lines between the left and right columns to find the correct translations.

```
S G L H E W V E R K E H R S E Y
I O F A H R B A H N H M D L A E
O Q E L R D O T I K M G L L W I
P D P E N A L L R O U E T L N N
R A A O Y N O I T A T S S A G B
L R R W N S A O H S F B Z F I A
L R K K A E R U K C V F Y N S H
A O I G P C W N T R S T I U P N
P T N E Y L A A B O N P B C O S
O O G C D T A E Y E M Z P U T T
T M L A L S S T D S N O V O S R
S E O U E T B I Z V T Z B V T A
S R T T P E C H G M S R I I S S
U H D O M C S T R A S S E N L S
B U S H A L T E S T E L L E O E
E R V T R A F F I C L I G H T W
```

AUTOMOBILE	EINBAHNSTRASSE
ACCIDENT	UNFALL
BUS	BUSHALTESTELLE
BUS STOP	VERKEHR
GAS STATION	BUS
GASOLINE	PARKPLATZ
LANE	AUTO
MOTORCYCLE	FAHRBAHN
ONE-WAY STREET	BENZIN
PARKING LOT	AMPEL
ROAD	TANKSTELLE
STOP SIGN	MOTORRAD
TRAFFIC LIGHT	STOPPSCHILD
TRAFFIC	STRASSE

Review Time: Draw lines between the English word on the left and the corresponding translation on the right. Refer back to the original puzzle if you need help.

```
P B L F A H R R A D Ö F Z U G O
O P O L I C E C A R I T D E U W
L A B A N F B N T R S R R N E U
I N I O T I U E E E E K T A Z N
Z Z C S S N A T N T N E C L R N
E E Y Y A C R R P A R Q S P H I
I R C K E U H O T S F U T R A A
F D L N C T C U E S B O S I F Ö
A E E K A I S E L L O O U A H E
H R H N L L B U O B G Z B H C H
R E E E F O U O B N U E M I S F
Z N H T O Ä H B H W A S A I Ö T
E I H T O C H A M U A C R S L F
U W E T S I B R C A O Y I L I T
G U E Z G U L F E R R Y N D E E
H R E T T U N G S W A G E N R O
```

AIRPLANE	LÖSCHFAHRZEUG
AMBULANCE	SCHULBUS
BICYCLE	BOOT
BOAT	UNTERSEEBOOT
CANOE	ZUG
FERRY	FÄHRE
FIRE TRUCK	HUBSCHRAUBER
HELICOPTER	U-BAHN
POLICE CAR	POLIZEIFAHRZEUG
SCHOOL BUS	RETTUNGSWAGEN
SUBMARINE	PANZER
SUBWAY	KANU
TANK	FAHRRAD
TRAIN	FLUGZEUG

Review Jumble: The translations in the word list below have been scrambled. Draw lines between the left and right columns to find the correct translations.

```
S G D T D P J A P A N I S C H H
H H D P J I T A L I E N I S C H
E T C P O L I S H S R Ö E S S C
B E T H R D G T E L L O I Y I S
R H F D E E E U A T Ö B H H N I
E C O R R B G U A L A U C S A S
W S E M E U R E T R I S S I E Ö
Ä I A C T N S Ä A S I A I L R Z
M N G R I E C H I S C H N G O N
W A O H N B T H S S S H L N K A
O P N A T Ö A U Ö P C T O E N R
F S P D T S R R A E S H P R A F
M A N D A R I N A I S S U R E I
J G H G O R I U G L O K E E R G
E T R H C S I S E I G U T R O P
W H V Ä H E E N G L I S C H K I
```

ARABIC	MANDARIN
ENGLISH	ENGLISCH
FRENCH	ITALIENISCH
GERMAN	SPANISCH
GREEK	GRIECHISCH
ITALIAN	JAPANISCH
JAPANESE	PORTUGIESISCH
KOREAN	ARABISCH
MANDARIN	RUSSISCH
POLISH	FRANZÖSISCH
PORTUGUESE	KOREANISCH
RUSSIAN	POLNISCH
SPANISH	HEBRÄISCH
HEBREW	DEUTSCH

Review Time: Draw lines between the English word on the left and the corresponding translation on the right. Refer back to the original puzzle if you need help.

```
T T O N N A M R E M M I Z A H R
A K P O L I C E O F F I C E R E
T E A C H E R T E T S T R E N T
E T T Z R A N H A Z O U L G N S
E I D B E N E G E R E L I Q N E
C H S O Y W M I R I E N I A A W
A C C R W A E F N T E T I P M H
R R G E A L T E S E Z C S V R C
P A C R L T G R R U I R D J H S
E U E H E N A I R R H B A S E N
N E N E I D F F T C W O O E W E
T U I L T T F C O D O C T O R K
E D R O E L E K T R I K E R E N
R K L S A L T C W E O C N T U A
D I E U E D E N T I S T K O E R
P O L I Z I S T X A J C H E F K
```

ACTOR	INGENIEUR
ARCHITECT	ANWALT
CARPENTER	DARSTELLER
CHEF	PILOT
DENTIST	ARCHITEKT
DOCTOR	LEHRER
ELECTRICIAN	FEUERWEHRMANN
ENGINEER	KOCH
FIRE FIGHTER	KRANKENSCHWESTER
LAWYER	ARZT
NURSE	ELEKTRIKER
PILOT	ZAHNARZT
POLICE OFFICER	ZIMMERMANN
TEACHER	POLIZIST

Review Jumble: The translations in the word list below have been scrambled. Draw lines between the left and right columns to find the correct translations.

```
H R A R Ä N N D C X T S I T R A
L E E J E N A I C I T I L O P C
H J F T S I N I R O L I A T O C
D D K R Ä A B E C I A B N Ä L O
Q A H Ü H T C R P I A B O N I U
A R M C N N I G A P S K Z Z T N
E R E E A S T N R B L U R E I T
A M E D C S T O A E P R M R K A
I T A G I H F L M S S O U R E N
Ä N H R Z E A P E E L S S E R T
A T O X S T N N D R O S I B E S
D L I S H E E H I E F E K R H I
F Ä O L R E S M C K N F E A C R
N R E B M U L P T S E O R B T O
O T B U C H H A L T E R T H U L
E N A V T R E L T R O P S H B F
```

ACCOUNTANT	BARBIER
ARTIST	KLEMPNER
ATHLETE	SCHNEIDER
BARBER	POLITIKER
BUTCHER	PROFESSOR
DANCER	KÜNSTLER
FLORIST	SANITÄTER
MECHANIC	FLORIST
MUSICIAN	BUCHHALTER
PARAMEDIC	SPORTLER
PLUMBER	TÄNZER
POLITICIAN	MECHANIKER
PROFESSOR	MUSIKER
TAILOR	METZGER

Review Time: Draw lines between the English word on the left and the corresponding translation on the right. Refer back to the original puzzle if you need help.

```
O I L T T E T Ü Ü H D S T P S I
R E H C S I F I S H E R M A N O
I S L L E L S O L D A T H E S N
O A A V N N S R E N T R Ä G S Y
H D J R E Z T E S R E B Ü V R Z
R J O U R N A L I S T S T E D P
E E U Ä F E A N O I T Z V T R H
K T R A J T I L F T R I E E E A
E O N H O E D R R A R V N R I R
H B A R A I W I R D R E L I L M
T T L D E F W E I A D M S N E A
O S I R D D I X L R C H E A W C
P O S T N T A X A E D L Ü R U I
A P T A R T I G A V R A I I J S
E F L I G H T A T T E N D A N T
R E T I E L G E B G U L F N M S
```

FARMER	JUWELIER
FISHERMAN	JOURNALIST
FLIGHT ATTENDANT	SOLDAT
GARDENER	FISCHER
JEWELER	TAXIFAHRER
JOURNALIST	TIERARZT
MAIL CARRIER	ÜBERSETZER
PHARMACIST	FLUGBEGLEITER
SOLDIER	APOTHEKER
TAXI DRIVER	GÄRTNER
TRANSLATOR	POSTBOTE
VETERINARIAN	LANDWIRT

Review Jumble: The translations in the word list below have been scrambled. Draw lines between the left and right columns to find the correct translations.

```
A A T M T R S S S Y W N E L T S
J S A H E T N U T P E N A T L T
M U L L M R H N S P E O N N E U
E D P O O S K O T D A E A A T E
T M O I K U I U N M F I B S A D
S N J N T N N O R G N G E I S I
Y R U C R E M N E A Y H D C P O
S E P O Z V R N P D N A C C R R
N C I W T R R S S H R U D W E E
E O T T I U O D U T S I S E J T
N E E O T N L H K N O R E N R S
N U R A N U S P A R E T A R C A
O E S E S R L T E U A V I M D P
S E O R A U E T E H T R A E E
I E E M T E S L I A A T E M O C
D P S O L A R S Y S T E M R F T
```

SOLAR SYSTEM	SATURN
MERCURY	ASTEROID
VENUS	VENUS
EARTH	JUPITER
MOON	SONNENSYSTEM
MARS	MERKUR
JUPITER	KRATER
SATURN	SONNE
URANUS	MOND
NEPTUNE	NEPTUN
PLUTO	MARS
SUN	KOMET
CRATER	URANUS
ASTEROID	PLUTO
COMET	ERDE

Review Time: Draw lines between the English word on the left and the corresponding translation on the right. Refer back to the original puzzle if you need help.

```
E N I R U O B M A T E H E R M E
T N O I N I R U B M A T O E H U
A N O H P O X A S L U N Ö A I B
H A E B L F G P T L A C A L D A
A I C L M P L E F I V D E D F C
R B E Ö I O N Ü P G U E I L T I
F C U P T U R A G R T G E N L N
E Ö E T A A D T Ü E A L N Ü T O
R S N S E K T U P H L H I F P M
R E O U A K C M D V I O L I N R
A P H D B O O N L E M M O R T A
T E P M U R T A H A L R I E I H
I E O L T D E D R U M S V R M H
G A X G Ö E N Ü T I T F A I E F
N N A C C O R D I O N T S C H H
S S S M U N D H A R M O N I K A
```

ACCORDION	AKKORDEON
BAGPIPES	SAXOPHON
CELLO	DUDELSACK
DRUMS	GITARRE
FLUTE	TROMMELN
GUITAR	TROMPETE
HARMONICA	FLÜGEL
HARP	HARFE
PIANO	MUNDHARMONIKA
SAXOPHONE	TUBA
TAMBOURINE	CELLO
TROMBONE	VIOLINE
TRUMPET	TAMBURIN
TUBA	POSAUNE
VIOLIN	FLÖTE

Review Jumble: The translations in the word list below have been scrambled. Draw lines between the left and right columns to find the correct translations.

```
T Y Y Ö C O N F I D E N T N G G
C H D P D E S S A R R A B M E O
A S C D P N H H S E I E A L D S
V N R S Q A A C T N S E A K U E
E O S H A C H H I O O N T R N L
R I A U O R C I R L G I P T X B
L T D T O Ü R G V W K R T Ö L S
E O D C H V T E E O I C W O H T
G M K C E H R I B S I C Ü Y M B
E E S G A W L E E Ü B O T L T E
N W Ö I I T E D N O R N E S G W
W O R R I E D A R E Ü F N Ö Ü U
Ö T R U E Ö K E P R O U D V E S
A T O A R O D E R A C S A R I S
A C Y R G N A A U F G E R E G T
Z L O T S E X C I T E D H N T A
```

EMOTION	NERVÖS
HAPPY	EMOTION
SAD	VERLEGEN
EXCITED	GLÜCKLICH
BORED	ÜBERRASCHT
SURPRISED	TRAURIG
SCARED	GELANGWEILT
ANGRY	ERSCHROCKEN
CONFUSED	STOLZ
WORRIED	SELBSTBEWUSST
NERVOUS	SCHÜCHTERN
PROUD	BESORGT
CONFIDENT	VERWIRRT
EMBARRASSED	AUFGEREGT
SHY	WÜTEND

Review Time: Draw lines between the English word on the left and the corresponding translation on the right. Refer back to the original puzzle if you need help.

```
O H G U O C I N F E K T I O N Ä
Ä T U H L T X Y G R E L L A N E
L H D S S L S O N I G A S A M A
L E I A T P A O P R T E U W A K
A A A R M E S F I N N S I I O N
F D R A T E N P N B E N N P N K
H A R G B S P O L A D K F R R G
C C H L N E S U I P G S C Ä R A
R H E J I U T E O T C A M I Ü L
U E A D E E T C T H C P L B H H
D Ü G L N A K L M E F E E H A C
S T R O K E A E Ä E B L F T C S
M I Ä C N E R F S K K A D N H S
R E V E F Z A L L E R G I E I U
D I A B E T E S I U C E V D Ü A
F P S N D A O T F I E B E R N R
```

ALLERGY	ALLERGIE
CHICKENPOX	HUSTEN
COLD	KOPFSCHMERZEN
COUGH	GRIPPE
CRAMPS	KRÄMPFE
DIABETES	ERKÄLTUNG
DIARRHEA	FIEBER
FEVER	DURCHFALL
FLU	WINDPOCKEN
HEADACHE	NASENBLUTEN
INFECTION	DIABETES
NAUSEA	AUSSCHLAG
NOSEBLEED	SCHLAGANFALL
RASH	INFEKTION
STROKE	ÜBELKEIT

Review Jumble: The translations in the word list below have been scrambled. Draw lines between the left and right columns to find the correct translations.

```
A B H V W H E X A R G K Y Ä D Y
G E U E D N U W T T I N H C S R
N O I R R M T V I R U S E P N E
E K H S N Z Ä T L M V E E B E Ä
Z X C T P O I P R E L L U N G A
R E M A S E R N R A I S U H I E
E M H U T F L B F P P A R R E I
M I Z C D T R I E A R E E F F A
H G E H A E A A P N R M O F C X
C R T U N H C T C E Ä K B U A R
S A I N O L C N R T S R T E Y E
N I U G S L I A L A U P G S Ä D
E N I P U A D E M C E R M I D Ä
G E M R R F E R H O H H E U M Z
A U H P I N N A M H T S A R M A
M I S U V U T A M H T S A B O H
```

ACCIDENT	VERBRENNUNG
ASTHMA	HERZINFARKT
BRUISE	MIGRÄNE
BURN	VIRUS
CUT	BRUCH
EPILEPSY	SCHNITTWUNDE
FRACTURE	MUMPS
HEART ATTACK	EPILEPSIE
MEASLES	VERSTAUCHUNG
MIGRAINE	UNFALL
MUMPS	MASERN
SPRAIN	PRELLUNG
STOMACH ACHE	MAGENSCHMERZEN
VIRUS	ASTHMA

Review Time: Draw lines between the English word on the left and the corresponding translation on the right. Refer back to the original puzzle if you need help.

```
F R S Ä T H A O H S T L E N A S
G W L S O E K Ä T O L T Ä A E E
N H O W F A R E L O W M D T M T
A A O I A H I R R H D M E H P S
B T N W T R E Y Y E T L U H L I
I T N R A W U N F O H E O C E T
O I E H H R A M E S A W A W H Ä
R M F O W M E L A T N I H Ä U P
A E L L W D E Y E L E E D I O S
W I E O E I W W O I N W D D Y E
D S H Y V B E C A U S E E O N I
N I R E H T I V N N D I H Ä A W
T T I A T S L R I E N T P T C L
S W M I E S L U L E B E Z A I W
E L U L E F D I O E L I D S N C
R I D S E T H E G E I W L A I T
```

BECAUSE	WIE
HOW	WANN
HOW ARE YOU	WER
HOW FAR	WEIL
HOW MANY	WIE SPÄT IST ES
HOW MUCH	WIE GEHT ES DIR
CAN YOU HELP ME	WARUM
WHAT	WO
WHAT TIME IS IT	WIE VIEL
WHEN	WIE WEIT
WHERE	kannst DU MIR HELFEN
WHO	WAS
WHY	WIE VIELE

Review Jumble: The translations in the word list below have been scrambled. Draw lines between the left and right columns to find the correct translations.

```
R E T I A W M S S N I K P A N O
D D E S S E R T I K H N I M E R
N D I N N E R E C O E C A F T A
A G T U G O L Ü Z T R I N A T D
H B Ü H R N T L T I N E E U E L
W R E I C S U E L C T P T S L M
I E B N H I I N O I E E S E I K
N A I Ü D V R U H S B E P T O N
E K R N R E R E I C R E T P T Ä
L F N E K S S E G T E A H D A R
I A S S E A P S K T G R N T M T
S S I S Q S R N E E P M E N Ü E
T T R E R A I T S N P U T I L G
S S M O O R T S E R P I A J D L
I E V R D L E G K N I R T H P H
S E W J G N U N E I D E B U T H
```

APPETIZER	MENÜ
BREAKFAST	DESSERT
DESSERT	ESSEN
DINNER	TRINKGELD
DRINK	FRÜHSTÜCK
EAT	GETRÄNK
LUNCH	ABENDESSEN
MAIN COURSE	BEDIENUNG
MENU	VORSPEISE
NAPKINS	SERVIETTEN
RESTROOMS	TOILETTEN
THE BILL	HAUPTGERICHT
TIP	MITTAGESSEN
WAITER	DIE RECHNUNG
WINE LIST	WEINKARTE

Review Time: Draw lines between the English word on the left and the corresponding translation on the right. Refer back to the original puzzle if you need help.

```
D O N O T D I S T U R B R V Y A
T E R I N T E R N E T H Ö O E U
O B B E C A B E T I U S L H O I
I Ö Ä G Z H E F V T L C U A I M
L E R T B E T L E T O H G N D O
E A E O E A P S S R E L G D U F
T A P W T L K T T C N Ü A T T Ü
T O A E T C E I I Ö G S G U S Ö
E N P L Ä K R V A O R S E C S L
N M T P N E R D I Ö N E Ö H S F
P Y E A M E T I U S I L N O E T
A G L M S N K Ü L M I A O T N R
P B I M R E C E P T I O N E T W
I Z O E Y K I D E C K E N L I J
E O T E N R E T N I B O Q Z F C
R Ö R E C I V R E S R E M M I Z
```

BED	DECKEN
BLANKETS	INTERNET
DO NOT DISTURB	FITNESSSTUDIO
GYM	SUITE
HOTEL	HOTEL
INTERNET	REZEPTION
KEY	ZIMMERSERVICE
LUGGAGE	TOILETTENPAPIER
RECEPTION	SCHLÜSSEL
ROOM	BETT
ROOM SERVICE	bitte NICHT STÖREN
SUITE	ZIMMER
TELEVISION	GEPÄCK
TOILET PAPER	FERNSEHER
TOWEL	HANDTUCH

Review Jumble: The translations in the word list below have been scrambled. Draw lines between the left and right columns to find the correct translations.

```
S P R A C H E N M E D I C I N E
O S H I S T O R Y C U H N O E L
G S E T H C I H C S E G D N A K
L C E N L E P T T M E O G N Y I
B I T G I A W F I N T I G H R S
I E S F R S Ä E I M N U P N E Y
O N I G A H U E Q E A O N T D H
L C O H C H U B E G S T M F N P
O E I S P R C R E O M E H A U T
G Ä E S W O I S L I D H Y H K K
I G T E U N S I N I R T G C D I
E A S R G M H O Z E O A O S R S
E E N E A P Ä I L D S M L T E U
N D U E C O N O M I C S O R Ä M
I N K Y R T S I M E H C I I I W
T M H A H S C I S Y H P B W E S
```

ART	CHEMIE
BIOLOGY	BIOLOGIE
BUSINESS	WIRTSCHAFT
CHEMISTRY	MUSIK
ECONOMICS	MATHE
ENGINEERING	INGENIEURWESEN
GEOGRAPHY	PHILOSOPHIE
HISTORY	MEDIZIN
LANGUAGES	PHYSIK
MATH	WISSENSCHAFT
MEDICINE	GESCHICHTE
MUSIC	GESCHÄFT
PHILOSOPHY	ERDKUNDE
PHYSICS	SPRACHEN
SCIENCE	KUNST

Review Time: Draw lines between the English word on the left and the corresponding translation on the right. Refer back to the original puzzle if you need help.

```
H M R P A R A L L E L A E N I L
E U U A N A D D I T I O N N N N
P L L G E O M E T R I E O E O O
E T E E A R I T H M E T I C I I
R I R L I D A T U A V S T G T T
P P Y H L W D E K O E P A L C A
E L R A O A N I L A E Y U E A K
N I T O S N R U T R R E Q I R I
D C E H Z N M A C I W T E C T L
I A M N C E O E P H O C B H B P
C T O N N E N I H A C N D U U I
U I E S M T R T S S Y I O N S T
L O G U A H A K S I H H E G T L
A N L G T I H E N A V E S R A U
R O E A R I T H M E T I K T E M
V D I V I S I O N T S Z D U H B
```

ADDITION	MULTIPLIKATION
AREA	PROZENTSATZ
ARITHMETIC	SUBTRAKTION
DIVISION	GEOMETRIE
EQUATION	GLEICHUNG
GEOMETRY	PARALLEL
MULTIPLICATION	SENKRECHT
PARALLEL	ADDITION
PERCENTAGE	VOLUMEN
PERPENDICULAR	ARITHMETIK
RULER	LINEAL
SUBTRACTION	DIVISION
VOLUME	BEREICH

Review Jumble: The translations in the word list below have been scrambled. Draw lines between the left and right columns to find the correct translations.

```
C I S E I R U N W A Y T L S J A
I N T E R N A T I O N A L H L B
T E E I R H L C U S T O M S A F
S F R E E U H Ä T T B Ä N F N L
E A M G T H T A N H N B O L O Ü
M H I A I I R R R D P T A U I G
O G N G D T E E A L I I T G T E
D U A G B T I N H P R S I S A N
U L L A N S K F A C E T C C N E
Ü F H B E Ü L S R C I D K H R B
E N E P N U S A U N N S E E E E
H T A F G P F R V V C A T I T H
E S T Z O T I O T I R D B N N B
S E E R O T O T D T R O P R I A
C U T N Y L L A N I M R E T H V
G E P Ä C K L F F O E K A T L I
```

AIRCRAFT	INLÄNDISCH
AIRPORT	REISEPASS
ARRIVALS	STARTBAHN
BAGGAGE	GEPÄCK
CUSTOMS	FLUGZEUG
DEPARTURES	ABHEBEN
DOMESTIC	ANKÜNFTE
INTERNATIONAL	INTERNATIONAL
PASSPORT	TERMINAL
RUNWAY	SICHERHEIT
SECURITY	ZOLL
TAKEOFF	FLUGSCHEIN
TERMINAL	FLUGHAFEN
TICKET	ABFLÜGE

Review Time: Draw lines between the English word on the left and the corresponding translation on the right. Refer back to the original puzzle if you need help.

```
O B E R E S L D G T E T N S N D
N U T Z P F L A N Z E N W N O G
N L R R E M R A F A H C S S P O
A D A B U E H D O E I D N S F A
Y E K R U T O E S P O R C T E T
U W T C T L H Ä H N C H E N R R
N N O Ä U R L A K L W O U E D I
B L R C T D A E H E E R T K S W
H T H E K T Y C I N K S N C S D
U V N A H A H N T Y O E E I Ä N
M Ä F F A M S E S O P E E H S A
E M E A R O Ä I R O R G H C H L
D A C Y R B L E E P E S T N A A
O C J R N E C B E I I T P M E M
E T O N B N A G Z G T K M L Z B
A I T Ä I W E H A I S M S U M L
```

BULL	TRAKTOR
CHICKEN	SCHAF
COW	NUTZPFLANZEN
CROPS	LANDWIRT
DONKEY	ENTE
DUCK	ZIEGE
FARMER	ESEL
GOAT	SCHWEIN
HORSE	TRUTHAHN
LAMB	STIER
PIG	HÄHNCHEN
ROOSTER	KUH
SHEEP	LAMM
TRACTOR	PFERD
TURKEY	HAHN

Review Jumble: The translations in the word list below have been scrambled. Draw lines between the left and right columns to find the correct translations.

```
N O T G S R I N E V U O S R R A
O M O N U M E N T E M K N E K Y
I A U C K I P I K R A P D I U P
T L R A A A D D S R P R I S N W
A S I S R M R E T E O N R E S N
M R S K T E C E B C F S I F T E
R I T I A N M O M O G Ü C Ü G D
O N R G E C E A R A O O H H A I
F E B L A O C M K D C K T R L U
N V I T E L A N U M E N U E E G
I U O E E T L R S N U R N R R R
T O U R I S T E U C O S G E I U
O S N O I T C E R I D M E D E O
M S N I U R S I C Y N A N U E T
R E G A H M I T M U S E U M M S
D R L W W B E O A A A U N A L E
```

ART GALLERY	RUINEN
CAMCORDER	PARK
CAMERA	REISEFÜHRER
DIRECTIONS	CAMCORDER
GUIDE BOOK	RICHTUNGEN
INFORMATION	MUSEUM
MAP	KARTE
MONUMENTS	KUNSTGALERIE
MUSEUM	SOUVENIRS
PARK	KAMERA
RUINS	TOURIST
SOUVENIRS	INFORMATION
TOUR GUIDE	MONUMENTE
TOURIST	REISEFÜHRER

Review Time: Draw lines between the English word on the left and the corresponding translation on the right. Refer back to the original puzzle if you need help.

```
L H U D V S V P G E E R U N W A
C N E E L L I R B N E N N O S H
L E V O H S A N D D I E N T S U
D M C A M O H R S B N F S O A M
S E S S A L G N U S G A R A S E
C R Z U S E U C U N N L R U N S
H C W N H S K R E D I E N T S D
A N E S U E F C B G M E C O S H
U E L C T E L U S I M O N U I E
F N L R N O R E E M I Z F H D F
E N E E C G R L E A W E C H A O
L O N E M M I W H C S A S I G T
F S A N D C A S T L E N R A I O
S N H L E V I E E B M H Z W V G
L Z S T E T S W S O L B B E D T
I R Y S O C G S E A T T P I N N
```

BEACH	SURFEN
BUCKET	HUT
HAT	MEER
OCEAN	SAND
SAND	WELLEN
SANDCASTLE	SCHAUFEL
SEA	EIMER
SHOVEL	SONNENBRILLE
SUN	SONNENCREME
SUNGLASSES	OZEAN
SUNSCREEN	STRAND
SURFING	SANDBURG
SWIMMING	SCHWIMMEN
WAVES	SONNE

Review Jumble: The translations in the word list below have been scrambled. Draw lines between the left and right columns to find the correct translations.

```
A O H T M H W U I H D M H C O S
M D T T R O C K E N A S S D R F
A B M R R C O T I U B C S Y H G
S U I R H H L E E H W E W A A Y
E D A G O O D B G G N E R E R I
Y N P U E R C I R M O D I D T O
V R S T I O H H O E R I G C T G
D W E G O O O M S Y I W E F H T
P W N Q O O J G S W T T O Z C S
E H W F E L D Y E O D S R P E R
E E S K O C O N R A M U S O L H
A U A A E A O L I O K A D P H G
H R R P L G L U G E Y A N I C S
W M O R M G I E T A L L A M S G
L T T U N A O H T O K T S A R
N O T D T N Z X X W B D N W K F
```

BIG	HART
SMALL	TROCKEN
WIDE	GUT
NARROW	KLEIN
TALL	ENG
SHORT	HOCH
HIGH	BREIT
LOW	NASS
GOOD	HOCH
BAD	GROSS
WET	WEICH
DRY	KURZ
HARD	SCHLECHT
SOFT	NIEDRIG

Review Time: Draw lines between the English word on the left and the corresponding translation on the right. Refer back to the original puzzle if you need help.

```
A L K T O A E H I L Y H E G A T
B U O A D L M A R O T S F H O O
N H F V L A U T E N C I T D E T
E C F Y S T C J H I C T M W M L
S S E G T E H B N N N R H C I L
S L N I E R E S U T E L P L W E
O A R E E U I S O U M P G R S N
L F T B I T S D E S R Y O F A H
H F U M S W S T H M I N O E A C
C A S R D R E C K I G I L T E S
S L O W G I L L I B H C M W E S
E A S I U C A B T P T L O R O B
G N H Q C H E A P S T O I L S B
B U F E S T O V N O I S Y N D D
R E A E V I S N E P X E A T Y E
I E P D N G S N H F L D M F I Z
```

FAST	BILLIG
SLOW	SAUBER
RIGHT	SCHNELL
WRONG	RICHTIG
CLEAN	LAUT
DIRTY	HEISS
QUIET	OFFEN
NOISY	DRECKIG
EXPENSIVE	RUHIG
CHEAP	LANGSAM
HOT	FALSCH
COLD	KALT
OPEN	TEUER
CLOSED	GESCHLOSSEN

Review Jumble: The translations in the word list below have been scrambled. Draw lines between the left and right columns to find the correct translations.

```
T A E I N F A C H R G N O R T S
N L G N I N N I G E B E D D L R
N A N I W E Ü H Ü W N U T I U H
D C A H W E S D Y H I D N R C U
T U F T K R A T S C W O E A I K
M L N E A R P K A S L E W F F X
D E A K K M L H G F L H V W F G
G S D N E O L L N I C T D A I Ü
Y T H G I L O I E S I W I N D S
T N B O U D V A E H W D D O O J
U D H F H R O E D H L O O T R S
A N S T T L J A E B L Q E H B D
I T Y S E Y E R H X V T I R F D
O A O F G N A E P N N R A H L Z
E O R D S U L E L A T C S L S N
A I L S F S W F H L S R E E Ü O
```

FULL	ENDE
EMPTY	VOLL
NEW	ANFANG
OLD	DÜNN
LIGHT	DICK
DARK	EINFACH
EASY	HELL
DIFFICULT	SCHWACH
STRONG	LEER
WEAK	ALT
FAT	NEU
THIN	SCHWER
BEGINNING	DUNKEL
END	STARK

Review Time: Draw lines between the English word on the left and the corresponding translation on the right. Refer back to the original puzzle if you need help.

```
D R J R X W L A S T C N T O W T
D N I E Ü O E T U O H T I W S Ä
O Y H E M H Z U O S S F E T B R
L O L I Ü T U O U C S O A S N E
Ü E T R E S L T H W N E A R D H
O M F L A R P N I N E N N I L H
N I U B E E E Ä H Ä E J S F A C
D Z E R E U A C T Ü Ü N T N E A
O O E E H Z F I B T I H F T T N
U H P E T O H E T T A H E W Ü A
T I R H I Ü E T U T D Y Ü O E T
S E E E W A Q C R H R Z L D N W
I D H E T A L S I T S W T L E E
D O R E A F E R N Ü A W L G E Z
E R O F E B A E O G S P L E C A
I T V E U S M E H P M A A N I E
```

NEAR	INNEN
FAR	AUSSEN
HERE	MIT
THERE	HIER
WITH	OHNE
WITHOUT	FERN
BEFORE	VORHER
AFTER	FRÜH
EARLY	SPÄT
LATE	DORT
INSIDE	NACHHER
OUTSIDE	ZULETZT
FIRST	NAH
LAST	ZUERST

Review Jumble: The translations in the word list below have been scrambled. Draw lines between the left and right columns to find the correct translations.

```
Y V H E E S N V W T E I C I K M
R W I I M E O G O L D O L W U A
C P E X O E Y G O N N R A N N S
E E N H E S T L D I O F I H S E
E A T I U C L A Y T M T R E T T
M N G I E O S S L A A Z E O S M
W G W L M T A S W L I L T B T O
Y S S M A N S K P P D O A A O R
W E I H D S F J A L E H M P F N
N E L L W I R D S T E E L R F E
I R V A B E A U W D N A S H T H
A O E D F E J M L L S G I E J L
L E R P N U R O A T T R E H O A
A N U O P E G L I N S L M N E T
D K T O C O N C R E T E V I E E
H S R T A O C W L A I R E T A M
```

CLAY	GOLD
CONCRETE	LEHM
COPPER	MATERIAL
DIAMOND	DIAMANT
GLASS	BETON
GOLD	SILBER
MATERIAL	SAND
METAL	STAHL
PLASTIC	KUPFER
PLATINUM	HOLZ
SAND	KUNSTSTOFF
SILVER	METALL
STEEL	GLAS
STONE	STEIN
WOOD	PLATIN

Review Time: Draw lines between the English word on the left and the corresponding translation on the right. Refer back to the original puzzle if you need help.

```
L L E L B R A M U I N I M U L A
H E U T T T O H B E G U M M I G
A E D K S O S A S D I N N D N I
T T X E I T U C L N Z E F M O D
S S S L R M M Z A U E X I R T R
L S H A W E A T N E M E C E T R
E S S O S D I R Z Q E I S B O U
D E L S A T O P E H N U N B C T
E L I E A B J S A K T E A U I U
E N L A A R O T O P S B E R M A
G I R O N T B D U I R O M R A M
P A P E R N H S E I L T W N R B
D T D O T L C E C N Z I E G E L
E S O R I E S K R R A T E H C E
E O M S N I R T I C B A B D D I
T P A A S N N G L I E N L Y T T
```

ALUMINUM	EISEN
BRASS	KERAMIK
BRICK	TITAN
CEMENT	BLEI
CERAMIC	ZEMENT
COTTON	MESSING
IRON	PAPIER
LEAD	BODEN
LEATHER	ALUMINIUM
MARBLE	ZIEGEL
PAPER	GUMMI
RUBBER	MARMOR
SOIL	EDELSTAHL
STAINLESS STEEL	BAUMWOLLE
TITANIUM	LEDER

Review Jumble: The translations in the word list below have been scrambled. Draw lines between the left and right columns to find the correct translations.

```
H E A I E E W I B R T U E R B B
T C H A E C H A M P A G N E R L
E A N A G I A H K I C H G I A O
N P C T H U E K B D S E A T N I
H P R E E J A T D H O N P A D I
C U O E T E E F F O C W M Y Y E
M C T D F E N N E R V D A E A K
X C W D A E N I W E T I H W N V
N I E W S S I E W W F L C R R K
I N I I W E O H A D A F A I R L
G O N B O E I S A T E A A E Z I
S S E L I S S K O K I R E K R M
W H I S K E Y D N A R B M E I E
Y G E E R N R U M T T H T L T Q
V D Y O N I C C U P P A C Z N F
D L E O L G B A D E W H T I N E
```

BEER	WODKA
BRANDY	RUM
CAPPUCCINO	CHAMPAGNER
CHAMPAGNE	WHISKEY
COFFEE	WASSER
GIN	BIER
JUICE	ROTWEIN
MILK	TEE
RED WINE	WEISSWEIN
RUM	MILCH
TEA	BRANDY
VODKA	SAFT
WATER	KAFFEE
WHISKEY	GIN
WHITE WINE	CAPPUCCINO

SOLUTIONS

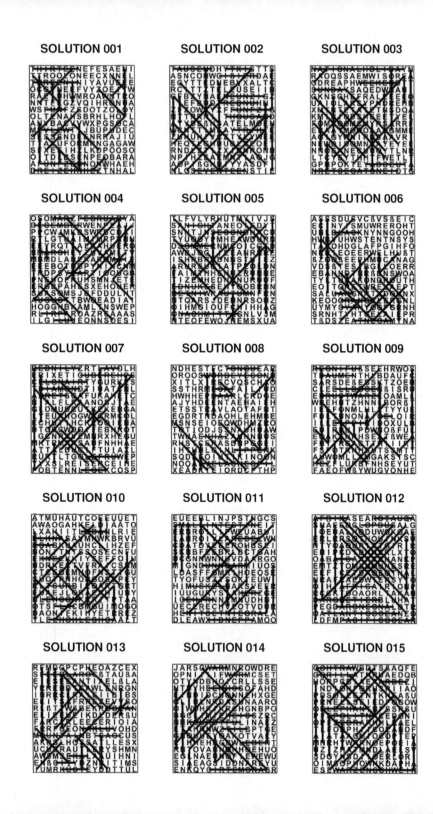

SOLUTION 001 SOLUTION 002 SOLUTION 003

SOLUTION 004 SOLUTION 005 SOLUTION 006

SOLUTION 007 SOLUTION 008 SOLUTION 009

SOLUTION 010 SOLUTION 011 SOLUTION 012

SOLUTION 013 SOLUTION 014 SOLUTION 015

SOLUTION 016

SOLUTION 017

SOLUTION 018

SOLUTION 019

SOLUTION 020

SOLUTION 021

SOLUTION 022

SOLUTION 023

SOLUTION 024

SOLUTION 025

SOLUTION 026

SOLUTION 027

SOLUTION 028

SOLUTION 029

SOLUTION 030

SOLUTION 031

SOLUTION 032

SOLUTION 033

SOLUTION 034

SOLUTION 035

SOLUTION 036

SOLUTION 037

SOLUTION 038

SOLUTION 039

SOLUTION 040

SOLUTION 041

SOLUTION 042

SOLUTION 043

SOLUTION 044

SOLUTION 045

SOLUTION 046

SOLUTION 047

SOLUTION 048

SOLUTION 049

SOLUTION 050

SOLUTION 051

SOLUTION 052

SOLUTION 053

SOLUTION 054

SOLUTION 055

SOLUTION 056

SOLUTION 057

SOLUTION 058

SOLUTION 059

SOLUTION 060

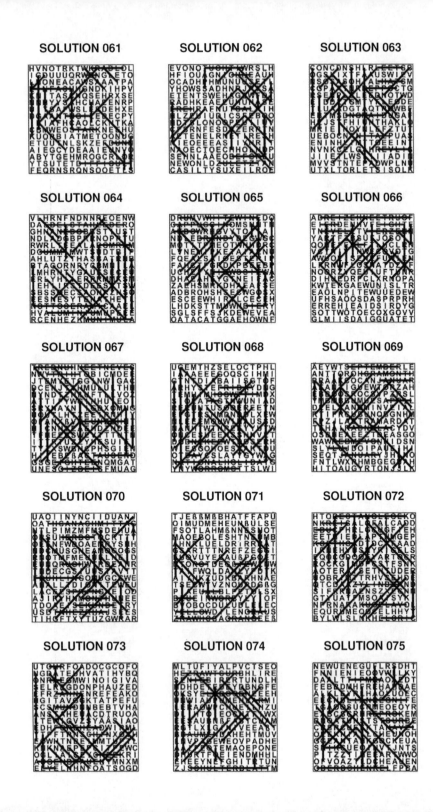

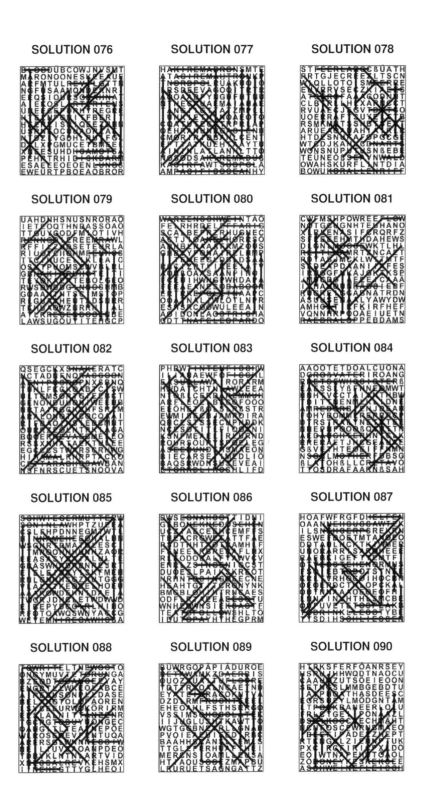

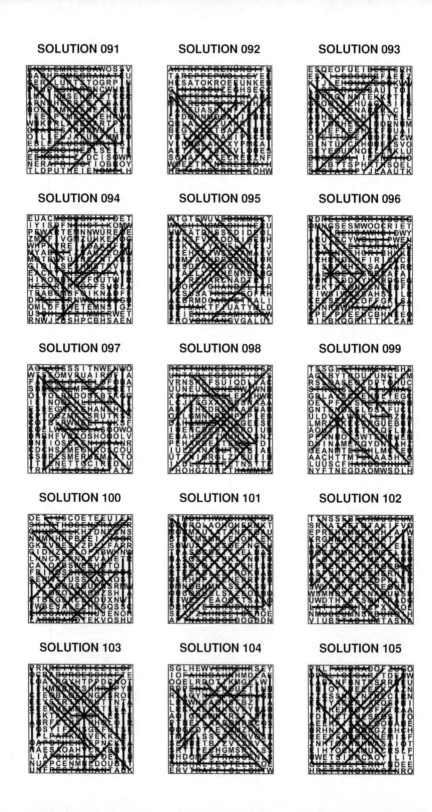

SOLUTION 091 SOLUTION 092 SOLUTION 093

SOLUTION 094 SOLUTION 095 SOLUTION 096

SOLUTION 097 SOLUTION 098 SOLUTION 099

SOLUTION 100 SOLUTION 101 SOLUTION 102

SOLUTION 103 SOLUTION 104 SOLUTION 105

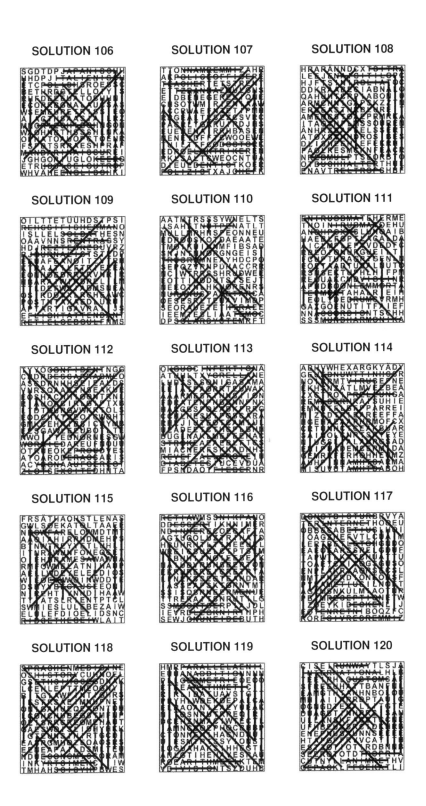

SOLUTION 106 SOLUTION 107 SOLUTION 108

SOLUTION 109 SOLUTION 110 SOLUTION 111

SOLUTION 112 SOLUTION 113 SOLUTION 114

SOLUTION 115 SOLUTION 116 SOLUTION 117

SOLUTION 118 SOLUTION 119 SOLUTION 120

SOLUTION 121

SOLUTION 122

SOLUTION 123

SOLUTION 124

SOLUTION 125

SOLUTION 126

SOLUTION 127

SOLUTION 128

SOLUTION 129

SOLUTION 130

Wordsearch Books by David Solenky

Language Series
Learn French with Wordsearch Puzzles
Learn German with Wordsearch Puzzles
Learn Hungarian with Wordsearch Puzzles
Learn Italian with Wordsearch Puzzles
Learn Polish with Wordsearch Puzzles
Learn Portuguese with Wordsearch Puzzles
Learn Romanian with Wordsearch Puzzles
Learn Spanish with Wordsearch Puzzles
Learn Swedish with Wordsearch Puzzles
Learn Turkish with Wordsearch Puzzles

Baby Name Series
Baby Name Wordsearch Puzzles
Baby Boy Name Wordsearch Puzzles
Baby Girl Name Wordsearch Puzzles

Made in the USA
Columbia, SC
09 December 2019

84595801R00080